PRO SPORTS CAR RACING
in America 1958-1974

Dave Friedman

MBI Publishing Company

First published in 1999 by MBI Publishing Company, 729 Prospect Avenue, PO Box 1, Osceola, WI 54020-0001 USA

MBI Publishing Company books are also available at discounts in bulk quantity for industrial or sales-promotional use. For details write to Special Sales Manager at Motorbooks International Wholesalers & Distributors, 729 Prospect Avenue, Osceola, WI 54020-0001 USA.

Library of Congress Cataloging-in-Publication Data
  Friedman, Dave.
     Pro sports car racing in America, 1958–1974 / Dave Friedman.
      p.   cm.
     Includes index.
     ISBN 0–7603–0618–4 (hardback : alk. paper)
     1. Automobile racing—United States—History. 2. Automobile racing—United States—History Pictorial works. 3. Sports car events—United States—History.   I. Title.
     GV1029.15.F66   1999
     796.72'0973—dc21   99–32722

On the front cover: In sixteen short years, professional sports car racing had risen and fallen in the United States. In the beginning, racing for money was fun. Competing drivers and crews socialized and traveled together, the media had full access to the teams and drivers, and photographers were allowed to roam the circuit in search of that one special shot that would stand out among all of the others. But as it evolved, governing organizations that split and couldn't agree on rules, insurance companies, corporate sponsors, and television producers all entered the game; each weighing in heavily on the future of the sport. By 1974, the period of gentlemen racers had passed. As corporate sponsorship and large viewership emerged as the bottom line, the racing had also evolved into some of the fastest, most powerful struggles in motorsports. As an example, George Follmer, seen here racing a Porsche 917/10K (16) through the corkscrew at Riverside battled the entire year of 1973 to finish second to Mark Donohue in the overall series points.

On the frontispiece: Porsche turned up the heat in the FIA Manufacturers' Championship in 1969 when it debuted the soon-to-be-legendary Porsche 917 at the Nurburgring in May. In America, the 917s first made their first appearance in February 1970 at Daytona. Though 917s would eventually dominate sports car racing, these first few years saw teams sorting out the details. Suspension problems dogged the Porsche 917s at the 1970 Sebring race, and a fourth place overall was the best that they could achieve there. In this picture, the Redman/Siffert/Kinnunen Porsche 917 (14) is seen during a night pit stop late in the race. This car would not finish.

On the title page: "RS" means Rennsport! A trio of Porsche RS61s straighten a chicane during the 1961 Nassau Trophy Race. Basing it on the successful RSK Spyder, Porsche produced 16 of RS 61 in 1961, 12 of which went to the hands of private racers. Bob Holbert (seen here in his RS 61, number 14, with a modified nose), went on to win national championships in the SCCA E Sports Racing class in 1961 and 1962. Chuck Cassel's RS 61 (16) and Peter DaCosta in a Porsche RS 61 (26) race for position. Holbert finished 7th, Cassel finished 10th, and DaCosta finished 13th in this Nassau Trophy Race.

On the back cover: Top: Ahhhh. The glory years of American sports car racing are well-represented on this grid. Awaiting the start of a practice session at the June 1965 Player's 200 are Jim Hall's Chaparral 2 (66), Hugh P. K. Dibley's Lola T70 (5), Ludwig Heimrath's McLaren M1A (1), Walt McKay's Cooper-Ford (93), Bob Johnson's Shelby Cobra (33), Chuck Dietrich's Elva BMW (57), Gary Gove's Cheetah-Chevrolet (17), Joe Buzzetta's Elva Porsche (3), Wayne Kelly's Porsche Special (81), and Bob Slotemaker's Porsche 904 (10).

Lower left: Mark Donohue began driving for car-dealer and former sports car champion, Roger Penske, in 1966. Although Donohue didn't become involved in Porsche's Can-Am effort until late 1971, his influence was critical in helping the factory win consecutive titles in 1972 and 1973. In this dramatic color shot, the Penske crew is preparing to push Donohue away during a practice for the July 1973 Watkins Glen Can-Am.

Lower right: Roger Penske was one of the first American car drivers to acquire substantial industry support. Here, he is adjusting the mirror on his Cooper Zerex Special as he sits on the starting grid prior to the November 1962 Puerto Rican Grand Prix. The following year, Penske teamed with Augie Pabst to capture the GT class at Sebring.

Edited by John Adams-Graf

Designed by Rebecca Allen

Printed in China

Contents

Acknowledgments

Many thanks must be given to Tim Parker, Zack Miller, John Adams-Graf, and Jane Mausser at MBI Publishing Co., without whom this book would not have been possible. They are the people most responsible for making this book a reality and making my job easier. To all of them, a huge "thank you." A special thanks and love to Susan Claudius.

I also must take a moment to thank all of the teams, drivers, crew members, and track personnel for making the era that is the subject of this book such a wonderful one in which to be involved. It was truly an era like no other, and, watching what racing has become today, one realizes just how wonderful those memories really are. Racing was really fun then; competing drivers and crews socialized and traveled together, the media had full access to the teams and drivers, and photographers were allowed to roam the circuit at will in search of that one special shot that would stand out among all of the others. Most of all, racing was not run by insurance companies, corporate sponsors, and extremely rude television producers and crews who dictate when, where, and what time a race will start. Courtesy abounded among the photographers and the media. If a photographer was first to a spot, he or she got first choice of the best position and was never pushed out of the way by some last-minute-arriving television camera crew, as they are today. Yes, things were different then, and I'm glad that I was there.

—Dave Friedman

Foreword

When I started racing my Triumph TR3 in 1954, sports car racing in America was strictly a gentleman's amateur sport. At that time, there was no thought of any professionalism being associated with our sport. It wasn't until 1958, when the United States Auto Club (USAC) started its professional road racing championship, that several of us realized that we could make some money doing what we liked to do. Bob Holbert, Fred Winridge, George Constantine, John Fitch, and several other East and West Coast drivers and I began to participate in the USAC races, much to the consternation of the SCCA, which didn't want any of its drivers racing for money. We tried to explain to John Bishop, Jim Kimberly, and the rest of the SCCA board members that the only way that many of the new tracks that were opening up around the country were going to stay in business was to hold a professional-quality event in which all of the big-name drivers and teams would appear. SCCA didn't want to hear any of that, and they decided to make an example of Bob Holbert and me by pulling our licenses so that we couldn't compete in their events. That situation all came to an end in 1959 when the Milwaukee Region of the SCCA was preparing to hold a national race at Meadowdale, and the regional executive of that region read the fine print in the rule book. It stated that anyone with an FIA license could be invited to participate in an amateur event; therefore, those of us who had been banned the year before didn't need SCCA licenses to race. The Board of Directors then sat down and worked out a compromise, and by the end of the year, it wasn't a problem any more.

The luckiest day of my life occurred in 1959, when Harry Heuer called my dealership looking for Paul O'Shea. Paul was staying with me at the time, and Harry wanted him to drive his team's new Scarab, which he had just acquired from Lance Reventlow. Paul wasn't there at the time, and I told Harry that he had just signed a deal with Bill Sadler and wouldn't be available, but that I was. I tested at Meadowdale that week and I got the ride. That was the beginning of my serious racing career. After driving for the Meister Brauser team for two seasons, I went on to drive for Briggs Cunningham and John Mecom before retiring at the end of the 1965 season to enter the family business.

What a joy it was to race during that era. The camaraderie, the cars, the fans, and the circuits all made it something very special. We were all friends during that period of time, and we all traveled together, roomed together, helped each other out at the track, and partied together after the race. It was a time when corporate sponsors, television producers, and insurance companies didn't dominate the weekend, and the driver and his crew could enjoy some of the atmosphere surrounding the event. Those times and those people are among my most cherished memories, and racing will never be like that again.

I am very happy to be able to write the foreword to this book because I have known Dave Friedman and his photographs for more years than I care to remember. Dave not only does great work, but he has been a good friend and, most of all, he was there when all of the events described in this book happened.

Enjoy the book. I know I will.

Augie Pabst

Augie Pabst
May 1999

The Beginning

By 1958, we were tired of racing for free, and many of us felt that we should be able to make a living by racing sports cars professionally in the U.S." Dan Gurney made that statement to me several years ago, and it illustrates the prevailing feeling among many of the country's best and most talented road racers of that era.

For many years, the Sports Car Club of America (SCCA) had resisted any thought of running professional races, fighting to keep the sport on an amateur level in spite of its continued growth in popularity. Racing competitive sports cars at the amateur level was a very expensive proposition. Without some kind of financial consideration or a wealthy patron, many of the top racers felt that they could not afford to compete at a level that was necessary to win.

George Constantine, driving his ex-factory Aston Martin, won the first two USAC professional races in 1958. Those races were run at Lime Rock, Connecticut, and Marlboro, Maryland.

Most of the top-ranked drivers sensed that sports car racing was in danger of becoming dormant and that it was time for the sport to proceed to the next level. Drivers like Dan Gurney, Phil Hill, Masten Gregory, Carroll Shelby, and Richie Ginther felt that the SCCA should pay prize and appearance money, as was the case in most other forms of motor racing. This created a serious division between the drivers and the SCCA, which was adamant that the sport remain amateur.

It was during this time that the United States Auto Club (USAC), the sanctioning body of the championship trail for Indianapolis-type cars and numerous midget, sprint, and stock car races, saw an opportunity to broaden its horizons by venturing into the fast-growing popularity of road racing. In 1958 the USAC created a professional division for road racing. When the SCCA heard of the USAC expansion, the organization promptly announced that it would ban any driver from further SCCA competition if he participated in a USAC-sanctioned professional race. When most of the top sports car drivers defied the ultimatum and competed in the USAC events, the SCCA backed down and dropped its threatened ban. What

Chuck Daigh works on a Chevrolet engine that would soon power one of the two magnificent Scarab sports cars that would dominate professional sports car races by year's end. The engine, shown here, is running on the dyno at the Reventlow shop in Venice, California.

The Chevrolet-powered Scarab, introduced in mid-1958, was heavily campaigned in California and by the end of the year in Nassau, the Bahamas, and the rest of the West Coast. It was campaigned on the East Coast in 1959. It was one of the most beautiful and successful front-engine racing cars ever built.

the SCCA had failed to realize was that the growing popularity of road racing was causing the costs of staying competitive to escalate to a point that was fast becoming cost-prohibitive to the racers. The USAC understood that road racing was the original form of automotive competition. Furthermore, it agreed that entering the exotic machinery required in this type of racing was indeed very expensive.

On September 7, 1958, the first of four USAC-sanctioned road races that season was run at Lime Rock, Connecticut. George Constantine defeated a field of 16 entries in the debut event, driving his ex-factory Aston Martin. Constantine won the following race at Marlboro, Maryland. In late September, Joachim Bonnier became the first foreign driver to win a USAC road race when he drove a Maserati to victory at Watkins Glen. Chuck Daigh, driving a Reventlow Scarab, won the final race on the USAC schedule, the Los Angeles Times Grand Prix for Sports Cars at Riverside. The annual running of the Times Grand Prix became one of the richest and most anticipated sports car events of the year. Its record crowds helped propel professional road racing to astonishing heights never thought obtainable. Dan Gurney became the first USAC Road Racing champion in 1958.

Dan Gurney was a young, fast-rising California racer in 1958. He was also one of the loudest advocates for a professional racing circuit. Gurney's outstanding performances in the Arciero Brothers' 4.9-liter Ferrari in 1958 and early 1959 won him a contract with the factory Ferrari team.

By 1959, the USAC Road Racing Division reached its peak by expanding to 11 races. Drivers like Augie Pabst, Phil Hill, Ken Miles, Jim Jeffords, Richie Ginther, Rodger Ward, Lloyd Ruby, George Constantine, and Stirling Moss won races, and Pabst became the USAC champion. Total prize money paid by USAC that year was $94,958, up considerably from the $24,600 paid the previous season.

For 1960 only five road races were scheduled, at Road America, Wisconsin; Castle Rock, Colorado; Laguna Seca, California; and two at Riverside, California. Carroll Shelby became the USAC champion in his final year of driving competition, before being forced into early retirement by a heart condition.

Ken Miles won the 1961 USAC championship by winning one and placing well in the other four officially sanctioned races that year. Three of the four races were divided into two heats, with the Times Grand Prix at Riverside, with no heats, being the notable exception. Lloyd Ruby, Augie Pabst, Bob Holbert, Jack Brabham, and Stirling Moss also won races that year.

By 1961, professional road racing had grown to a point where the crowd for the annual Times Grand Prix reached a track record of over 75,000, and the second year event at Laguna Seca pushed that track crowd record to almost 50,000. These two West Coast races set the standard for professional events to come by paying top appearance money in order to attract the best teams, drivers, and cars. The public responded by buying tickets in record numbers. In 1961 the Mosport circuit in Canada organized the first two professional sports car races ever run in that country. Stirling Moss won the Player's 200 in June, and Canadian-born Peter Ryan defeated an international field to win the Canadian Grand Prix for Sports Cars in September. These Canadian races drew unexpected crowds of over 40,000 fans for each of the two events—this in spite of questionable weather.

Phil Hill in a Ferrari 412 MI (2) and Chuck Daigh in a Scarab (5) staged a crowd-thrilling, wheel-to-wheel battle for the lead during the early laps of the 1958 Times Grand Prix. Hill was forced out of the race with four laps to go, leaving Daigh to go on to an unexpected win. Dan Gurney finished second. An international field of cars for that race drew an unexpected crowd of 70,000 people to Riverside. The large number of spectators completely overwhelmed the facilities.

Ken Miles (left) wishes Chuck Daigh (right) good luck prior to the start of the first *Los Angeles Times* Grand Prix in October 1958. The Times Grand Prix, held at Riverside, was the first of the topnotch professional races that would soon proliferate across North America. Scarab mechanic Harold Daigh, Chuck's brother, is in the center of the photograph.

Masten Gregory was one of the first Americans to race successfully in Europe in the 1950s. Gregory was also one of the major supporters of professional racing in the United States and, like Phil Hill, raced here when his schedule permitted.

Richie Ginther (left) and Jackie, his wife at the time, receive a trophy from Phil Hill at an awards ceremony in September 1958. Ginther and Hill (when his European schedule permitted) belonged to the tight-knit group of California drivers who battled the SCCA over professional racing.

A youthful Dan Gurney (right) receives congratulations from Carroll Shelby after winning the first USAC Road Racing Championship in 1958. Shelby would win the same championship in 1960.

One of the best things about the season-ending Nassau Speed Week was catching up with old friends not often seen during the year. Lance Reventlow (left, facing camera), Chuck Daigh (sitting against the 98 car), and Carroll Shelby (right, sitting on the ground) join others in a light-hearted discussion before practice.

Rarely did the two team RAI (Reventlow Automobiles Incorporated) Scarabs run this close together at any race, but they did on their way to a one-two victory at Laguna Seca in November 1958. Laguna Seca hosted its first professional race in October 1960 and would become one of the most popular stops on that circuit. Note that Chuck Daigh drives the right-hand-drive Scarab (5), while Lance Reventlow drives the left-hand version (16).

Having seen the success of the Times Grand Prix at Riverside the previous year, the rival *Los Angeles Examiner* decided to hold a professional race at Pomona in March 1959. Because a lot of appearance money was paid, many of the American and European stars showed up to compete. Dan Gurney's Ferrari 4.9-liter (69) leads Max Balchowsky's *Old Yeller* (70), Carroll Shelby's Maserati 5.7 (98), Chuck Daigh's Kurtis 500-Buick (6), Bill Krause's Maserati 4.5 (53), Jim Jeffords' Scarab (114), George Amick's Mercedes-Chevrolet (181), Wayne Weiler's Lister-Corvette (82), Sammy Weiss' Porsche RS (55), and Ken Miles' Porsche RS (50) during first lap action at Turn 3.

Chuck Daigh's Kurtis 500-Buick (6), Bill Krause's Maserati 4.5 (53), George Amick's Mercedes-Chevrolet (181), Wayne Weiler's Lister-Corvette (82), and Ken Miles' Porsche RS (50) in early lap action on the twisty Pomona track. Ken Miles was the overall winner in his Porsche.

Ron Flockhart's D Jaguar (127), Bruce Kessler's Sadler (3), Lloyd Ruby's Maserati-Chevrolet (46), Jim Rathmann's Ferrari 4.9 (88), Bob Oaker's Aston Martin (59), Bob Drake's Cooper (49), and Joe Playan's Porsche RS (29) show how close the action was at Pomona.

Augie Pabst leaps from his D-Type Jaguar during a fuel stop at Daytona. Note the original speedway grandstand and press box in the background.

Shortly after the Daytona International Speedway opened in February 1959, USAC ran an FIA-sanctioned 1,000-kilometer sports car race at the track in April. Running in reverse direction, George Constantine's Aston Martin (49) leads A. J. Foyt's Lister-Corvette (212) early in the race.

Pedro von Dory, Antonio von Dory, and Robert Mieres receive the winners' plaudits. This particular event was never run again, probably due to lack of interest.

Opposite, top: One of America's most famous competitors, Carroll Shelby, drove one of the Micro-Lube 4.5 Maseratis at Daytona.

Opposite, bottom: Pedro von Dory's Porsche RSK (86) leads the OSCA (38) of Ricardo Rodriguez through the infield of the new speedway.

The Kiwanis International service club decided that it too would run a professional sports car race, to raise money for charitable causes. The Kiwanis race at Riverside in July 1959 was not as successful as hoped and was never held again. In the crowded (for that era) pit area, the crews of John Edgar (foreground) and John von Neumann are hard at work.

Jack Flaherty embarrassed himself by parking this Lister Jaguar on top of the Turn 6 barrier and hay bales.

Opposite, top: Jim Jeffords' Scarab (10) leads Pedro Rodriguez's Ferrari TR (5) out of Riverside's Turn 9 as it looked in 1959.

Opposite, bottom: Chuck Daigh's John Edgar Special (98) leads Sammy Weiss' Porsche RSK (55) through the famed Riverside esses. Some of the rather sparse crowd attending the Kiwanis race can be seen in the background. Daigh finished sixth overall.

Rodger Ward was one of the first of America's great oval track racers to take to professional sports car racing. At the 1959 Times Grand Prix, Ward sits in the Leader Card Porsche RSK, but engine problems forced him to switch to a 4.4-liter Ferrari for the consolation race. Ward won that race but failed to finish the Grand Prix.

Stirling Moss never could resist a really good photo opportunity.

Actress June Wilkinson discusses race strategy with Ken Miles (left) and Otto Zipper. Wilkinson's rather obvious assets did not distract Miles too badly, because he went on to finish third overall in the Times race.

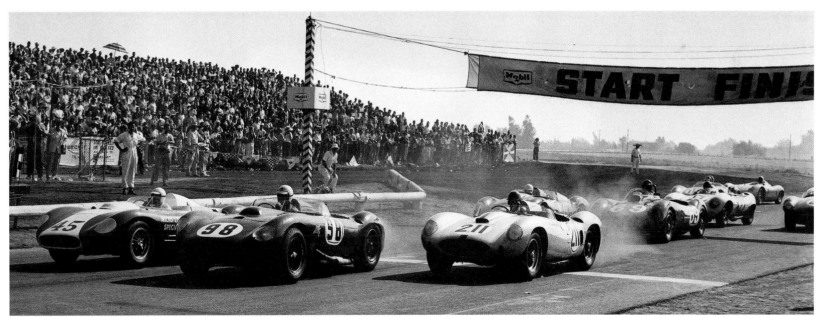

Chuck Daigh's Maserati 5.7 (98), Lloyd Ruby's Maserati 4.5 (45), and Richie Ginther's Ferrari 4.1 (211) race for Turn 1 during the first start of the 1959 Times Grand Prix. Phil Hill's Ferrari TR59 (2), Dan Gurney's Ferrari 4.9 (69), Bill Krause's D Jaguar-Chevrolet (27), Stirling Moss' Aston Martin DBR1 (28), Augie Pabst's Scarab (108), and Ken Miles' Porsche (50) give chase. Moments after this picture was taken, Gurney was rear-ended by Jack Graham's Chevrolet-powered Aston Martin, stopping the race. After a cleanup that took 35 minutes, the race was restarted without the damaged cars.

Chuck Daigh in his 4.5 Maserati (98) leads the eventual second place Grand Prix finisher Lloyd Ruby in his 4.5 Maserati (45) out of Turn 6. Lloyd Ruby was another one of the well-known oval track stars who loved racing in professional sports car events when his busy schedule allowed it.

Opposite: Stirling Moss in his Aston Martin DBR1 (28) and Phil Hill in his Ferrari TR59 (2) engaged in a furious race for second place while pursuing leader Richie Ginther. Moss lost oil pressure in his engine on the 26th lap, forcing him to retire from the race.

Jim Jeffords in his Scarab (10) leads Ricardo Rodriguez in a Porsche RSK (65) early in the race. Both cars failed to finish. Note the way that Riverside's famed Turn 6 looked in the late 1950s. Also note the proximity of the crowd to the race track. That luxury would soon change.

USAC oval track drivers Wayne Weiler in a Lister-Corvette (82) and Johnny Mantz in a Mercedes-Chevrolet (181) lead eventual third place finisher Ken Miles, driving a Porsche RSK (50). Note the radio whip antenna on Weiler's Lister. While a radio communication system in a racing car isn't given a second thought today, it was considered a novel experiment in 1959.

Phil Hill reacts in sheer delight as he feasts his eyes on the winner's share of the $20,000 purse. Eleanor von Neumann, Hill's sponsor, holds the check.

Two of the first Maserati Tipo 61 Birdcages to be seen in North America were delivered to Gaston Andrey (25) and Loyal Katskee (12) at Nassau in December 1959.

Dick Thompson (left), George Constantine, and General Motors' Bill Mitchell (right) enjoy a social chat during a pause in the December 1959 Nassau Speed Week practice.

A very young Dan Gurney, in the Camoradi USA Maserati Tipo 61, awaits the start of the 1959 Nassau Trophy race. Legendary Maserati chief mechanic Guerrino Bertocchi stands behind the car.

As a strong field gets way from the Le Mans start of the Nassau Trophy race, eventual race winner George Constantine (49) and Stirling Moss (3), both in Aston Martins, are left at the line. Also at the back of the pack are Wayne Burnett's Ferrari (94), Dan Gurney's Maserati Tipo 61 (20), Bud Gates' Corvette SR2 (102), Harry Blanchard's Porsche RSK (61), Bob Holbert's Porsche RSK (78), Richard Macon's Lotus 11 (7), Paul Richards' Fiat Abarth (81), and Lloyd Ruby's 4.5 Maserati (51).

Left: The *Los Angeles Examiner* moved its Grand Prix from Pomona to Riverside in April 1960. This was the second and final race that the *Examiner* ran in an effort to duplicate the event run very successfully by its Los Angeles rival, the *Times.* Max Balchowsky (left) and Dan Gurney confer before practice. Gurney drove Balchowsky's *Old Yeller II* in the Examiner Grand Prix and was leading on lap 40 when a blown engine put him out of the race.

World Champion Jack Brabham in his Cooper Monaco (3) leads Bob Drake, driving a Maserati Tipo 61 (49), past a packed grandstand in Riverside's Turn 6. Drake was the fastest qualifier and led until engine problems sidelined him on the 25th lap. Brabham ran well up in the field until overheating and carburetion problems caused him to spend five minute in the pits. He rejoined the race and finished 12th overall.

Ken Miles in a Porsche RS60 (50) laps Jack Eubank in a Talbot Special (161) while cresting Turn 7 at Riverside. This spot was one of the best, and most scenic, photographic positions at that track. Miles finished 3rd overall, and Eubanks finished 14th.

Driving the Camoradi USA Maserati Tipo 61, Carroll Shelby (98) drove a smart and steady race in the 1960 Examiner Grand Prix. His strategy paid off with a popular win. Shelby is seen here leading Pedro von Dory's Porsche RS60 (11) moments before von Dory flipped off the course in the esses, and was instantly killed.

A jubilant Carroll Shelby celebrates the final international win of his storied driving career. Shelby retired at the end of the 1960 season due to heart problems.

Carroll Shelby savors the moment in what would be the final win of his driving career. Before retiring as a driver, Shelby won the USAC championship in 1960.

Opposite, top: During the USAC professional sports car race held at Colorado's Continental Divide Raceway in June 1960, Carroll Shelby in his Scarab (2) leads Jim Hall's Maserati Tipo 61 (66), Loyal Katskee's Maserati Tipo 61 (12), and John Kilborn's Scarab (1). Shelby won in his only drive in a Scarab, followed to the finish by Kilborn and Hall. Katskee did not finish.

Opposite, below: The Meister Brauser Scarab team of Harry Heuer (2) and Augie Pabst (1) was always one of professional sports car racing's most popular teams. The team is seen on the infield of the beautiful Road America circuit near Elkhart Lake, Wisconsin, during the USAC race in July 1960.

A full starting grid sits ready to race at Road America. Carroll Shelby in *Old Yeller II* (10) and Augie Pabst in his Scarab (1) sit on the front row while Jim Jeffords' Maserati Tipo 61 (55), Harry Heuer's Scarab (2), Roger Penske's Porsche RS60 (6), and Loyal Katskee's Maserati Tipo 61 (12) line up behind. Jeffords won the race.

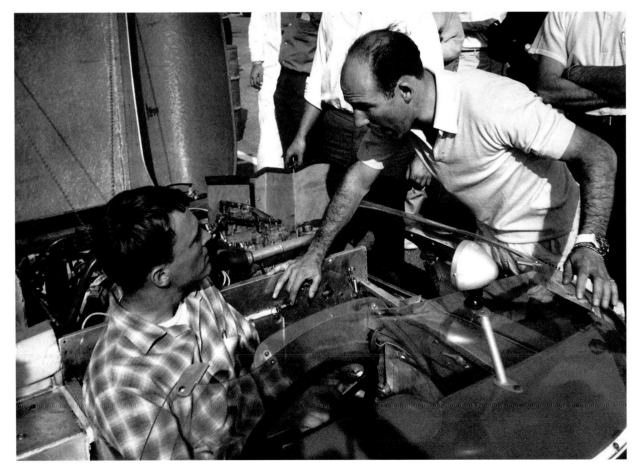

Dan Gurney (left) and Stirling Moss compare notes on the new Lotus 19 Monto Carlo. Moss and Gurney had the only two Lotus 19s in North America at the time of the 1960 Times Grand Prix.

Ken Miles (left), Jack Flaherty, and Roy Salvadori (right) share a moment in the Riverside pits before the start of practice.

Jack Brabham's E-Type Jaguar (60), Jay Chamberlain's Lotus 15 (152), and Loyal Katskee's Maserati Tipo 61 (12) await the start of the race. Brabham finished 10th in the Times Grand Prix, while Chamberlain and Katskee failed to finish.

Previous pages: Kurt Neumann behind the wheel of a Lotus Le Mans 11 (32), Jim Connor in a Maserati Tipo 61 (48), and Jack McAfee in a Porsche RS60 (88) prepare for qualifying.

This is how people used to watch the races before the building of scaffolds was outlawed for safety reasons. Occasionally the scaffolds would collapse due to poor construction and there would be significant injuries.

Jim Hall in his 5.7 Maserati (166) and Roger Penske in his Porsche RS60 (6) are ready to start. Jim Hall finished ninth, while Penske did not finish because of a blown engine.

Max Balchowsky rushes to complete drivetrain repairs to his *Old Yeller II* prior to the start of the first Pacific Grand Prix at Laguna Seca in October 1960. Bob Drake drove *Old Yeller* in the first heat, and Dan Gurney drove it in the second. Balchowsky's car retired from both heats with mechanical problems.

Dan Gurney (white sweater) watches as his Arciero Lotus 19 crew tries to complete flywheel repairs prior to the end of qualifying. Gurney asked for an extension of the qualifying session to allow his crew time to finish repairs. The USAC would not extend the qualifying session, and Gurney was not allowed to run the race.

Stirling Moss watches as his potential win at the Times Grand Prix goes up in smoke after only 10 laps. Moss was the race leader at the time of the fire.

Stirling Moss prepares to start the Pacific Grand Prix with his UDT-Laystall Lotus 19. Note the makeshift rollbar installed at the last minute by Moss' crew. Rollbars were not required in Europe at that time, but the strict USAC safety rules required them on all cars competing in American races.

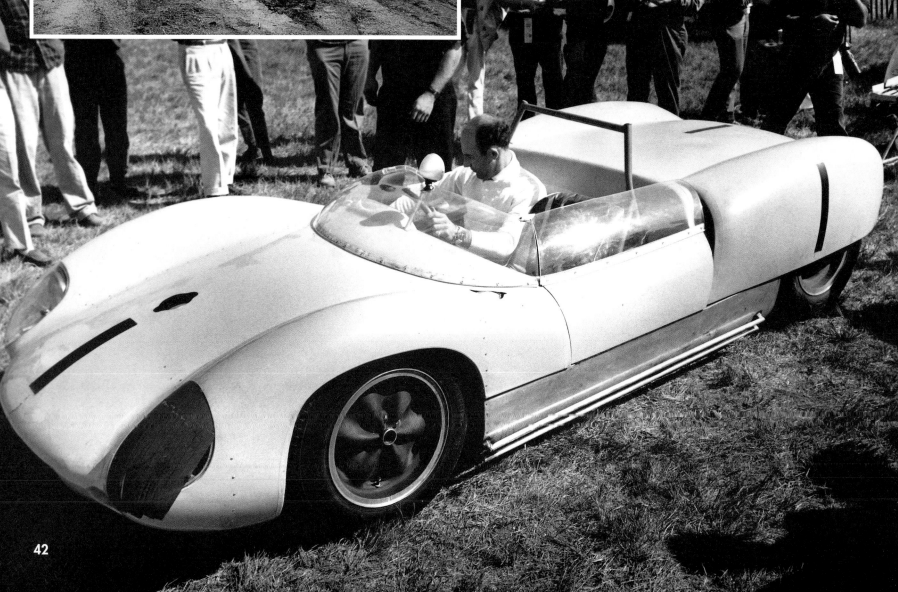

Jim Hall (48), Stirling Moss (1), and Bill Krause (53) battle for the Pacific Grand Prix lead. Moss was the overall winner, while Hall finished 3rd and Krause 10th.

These were the days when the spectators could really get close to the competitors. Unfortunately, in later years safety contraints changed all of that.

Stirling Moss wins the first professional race ever held at Laguna Seca in October 1960. Second place went to Carroll Shelby and third to Jim Hall.

Opposite, top: Carroll Shelby drove his final race in the J. Frank Harrison Maserati Tipo 61 at the Pacific Grand Prix. In spite of suffering from severe heart problems, Shelby managed to finish second overall.

Opposite, bottom: A very young Bruce McLaren drove his Jaguar E-Type (60) in his first of many professional sports car races in North America, at Laguna Seca in October 1960. McLaren finished 14th overall, while Loyal Katskee, driving a Maserati Tipo 61 (12) finished 21st.

Three of the best Porsche drivers of the era gather for a friendly discussion prior to the start of the July 1961 USAC Professional Sports Car race at Colorado's Continental Divide Raceway. Bob Holbert (left) won the race in his RS 61 while Scooter Patrick (center) finished fourth and Ken Miles (right) came in second. Miles would become the USAC road racing champion in 1961.

Chuck Sargent's Maserati Tipo 61 (21) and Ron Hunter's OSCA-Corvette (20) became "close friends" during the Continental Divide USAC race. Neither driver was injured.

I'll bet that no one has ever seen a Maserati Tipo 61 acting like a rally car in the dirt. Well, that's just what happened at the Pikes Peak Hill Climb in July 1961, when Don Skogmo drove his Birdcage up the hill with all of the skill and determination that one would normally associate with the likes of A. J. Foyt. Skogmo finished eighth overall in the very popular and competitive sports car division. Note where the very brave fans and lone photographer stand.

For the 1961 Times Grand Prix, the UDT-Laystall team brought two Lotus 19s to Riverside. Stirling Moss (standing behind the mechanic at the right) drove the Number 7 car, while Olivier Gendebien (in the dark sweater) drove the under-two-liter car in the background. Moss did not finish, but Gendebien finished sixth overall and won the under-two-liter class.

Augie Pabst in his Maserati Tipo 63 (60) leads Bill Krause's Maserati Tipo 61 (21), Bob Bondurant's Corvette (614), and Ricardo Rodriguez's Ferrari TR 61 (68) into Riverside's Turn 6 on a very hot and dusty day. None of these drivers finished.

Being a corner worker at a professional sports car race can be a dangerous profession, as this volunteer flag man found out when he was chased up a hill by an out-of-control Cooper Monaco driven by George Grinzewitsch. Fortunately, no one was hurt.

Roger Penske, driving his Cooper Monaco (16), chases Bill Krause's Maserati Tipo 61, Peter Ryan's Lotus 19 (83), and Chuck Daigh's Scarab (15) out of Riverside's Turn 6. Penske, who placed fourth overall, was the only one of these four drivers to finish the race.

Two-time World Champion Jack Brabham, driving a Cooper Monaco (4), and his Grand Prix teammate Bruce McLaren, also in a Cooper Monaco (6), thrilled a record crowd of 70,600 by staging a fantastic race. The two cars were seldom further apart than seen here. After numerous lead changes between the two, Brabham beat McLaren to the finish line by a mere 1.1 seconds.

This complicated, thin-tubed chassis shows why the Maserati Tipo 61 was called the "Birdcage" by the motor racing world. This car, being prepared for the Pacific Grand Prix at Laguna Seca, was owned and driven by Chuck Parsons.

One of the greatest of all Monterey, California, racing legends is based on an incident at the Mark Thomas Inn when Augie Pabst won a bet from Roger Penske and Walt Hansgen by driving his Hertz-rented Ford Falcon into the swimming pool of the above-mentioned hotel in 1961. It wasn't until the car hit the bottom of the pool that Hansgen realized that his camera was still in the trunk of the sunken vehicle and dove in to try to rescue it. Although the stunt was well received by all in attendance at the party, the hotel and car rental company didn't see the humor in it all. However, when both businesses realized how much free front-page publicity the incident generated, they quickly changed their tune.

A star-studded entry started the October 1961 Pacific Grand Prix at Laguna Seca. Stirling Moss in his Lotus 19 (1) leads the international field toward Turn 1, as Dan Gurney's Lotus 19 (96), Roger Penske's Cooper Monaco (16), Bruce McLaren's Cooper Monaco (6), Peter Ryan's Lotus 19 (83), Jim Hall's Chaparral 1 (66), and Jack Brabham's Cooper Monaco (4) chase Moss up the hill.

Roger Penske (16) and Stirling Moss (1) race neck-and-neck down the start-finish straight. Moss won the race, while Penske finished fifth.

USAC Road Racing Champion Ken Miles in his Porsche RS 61 (50) leads Dan Gurney in his Lotus 19 (96) entering Laguna Seca's Turn 8. Miles finished 11th while Gurney did not finish due to engine failure.

Stirling Moss takes the checkered flag for the second consecutive year at the October 1961 Pacific Grand Prix. Sadly, this would be the final win for Moss in North America, since he suffered catastrophic, career-ending injuries in a nonchampionship Formula One race at Goodwood the following April.

Harry Heuer's Scarab (22), Ken Miles' Porsche RS 61 (50), Chuck Parsons' Maserati Tipo 61 (110), and Jack McAfee's Porsche RSK (88) are in close pursuit of each other through Turn 7. Heuer did not finish, while Miles finished 11th, Parsons finished 6th, and McAfee finished 10th overall.

It was a great start for the December 1961 Nassau Trophy Race. Art Huttinger's Lister-Corvette (24), Norm Namerow's Corvette (72), Pedro Rodriguez's Ferrari TR 61 (2), Bob Publicker's *Old Yeller* (53), Jim Hall's Chaparral 1 (66), and George Reed's Ferrari TR 60 (93) all exploded off the line when the green flag fell.

Grant Clark (51) drives a Canadian-built Sadler at Nassau. The Sadler was one of the first successful rear-engine cars to be built from the ground up to accept an American V-8 engine. Was it a trend setter? You bet, but it was just a little ahead of its time and died due to lack of financial support.

Stirling Moss, Katie Moss, Graham Hill, and Dan Gurney enjoy one of the many parties that the Nassau Speed Week was known for. Nassau was better known for its social calendar than its racing—everyone looked forward to a "vacation."

Left: A proud Dan Gurney accepts the Nassau Trophy.

Opposite: Dan Gurney, driving a Lotus 19 (1), scored a spectacular record-setting win in the Nassau Trophy Race.

The Explosion

By the middle of the 1962 season, USAC had decided that it would not continue to conduct a separate road racing division starting in 1963. Could the reason have been that the SCCA, which had finally realized that professional sports car racing was here to stay, had announced that it would conduct its first professional series, the United States Road Racing Championship (USRRC), in 1963? The answer to that question may never be known, but what is known is that Roger Penske capped a banner year by winning the final USAC Championship, driving his controversial Cooper Formula One–based sports car, the Zerex Special. That car was one of the major stories of the year, and it showed the type of excellence and attention to detail that would become the Penske trademark for years to come.

Also in 1962, several of the grand touring cars that would contribute so much to the colorful racing history of the mid-1960s made their racing debuts. They were the Ferrari GTOs, Aston Martin Project Cars, lightweight Jaguar XKEs, Corvette Z06s, and Shelby American Cobras. The Ferrari team was in the midst of switching to rear-engine prototypes, and Lance Reventlow introduced a beautiful new rear-engine Scarab, which would become extremely successful in the hands of the John Mecom racing team. By the end of 1962, it was obvious to most of those in the know that the way to go in professional racing was with an American engine in the rear of a Cooper or Lotus chassis.

The big news in 1963 was the debut of the new *Fédération Internationale de l'Automobile* (FIA) and the SCCA-sanctioned professional sports car series known as the United States Road Racing Championship. This inaugural eight-race series was split into two championships: the Manufacturers' Championship for production-based cars, and the Driver's

Opposite: In February 1962, Carroll Shelby (background) built his first Cobra in the back of Dean Moon's racing shop. Working on a shoestring budget, Shelby persevered with his dream of building a high performance car that would challenge the well-established General Motors Corvette. Many people laughed at the idea and said that it would never work. Boy, were they in for a surprise.

It wasn't a professional race, but this race, the Cal Club (California Sports Car Club), at Riverside in February 1962 was one of the best, and closest, of the entire season. Bob Harris, driving a Campbell-Corvette Special (17), and Dave MacDonald, with a Simpson Corvette Special (00), ran closely, swapping the lead numerous times, until MacDonald finally prevailed to beat Harris by a few feet.

Masten Gregory (4) and Dan
Gurney (96), both in Lotus 19s,
were the stars of the show at the
June 1962 Players 200, held on
the beautiful Canadian circuit at
Mosport, Ontario, near Toronto.
Gurney won the first heat, with
Gregory finishing second. In the
second heat, Gregory took an
immediate lead and assured
himself of the overall win when
Gurney dropped out of the race
with mechanical problems.

Championship for modified cars. The first race was run at Daytona on February 3, 1963, and was won by Jim Hall. By the time the USRRC season was completed at Mid-Ohio in late September, Bob Holbert had won the Driver's Championship, and Shelby American, after a close early season battle with Ferrari, had won the Manufacturers' Championship. Cobra and Ferrari were now serious rivals.

The rise in the popularity of professional road racing was evident in the record number of international entries and the crowds that attended the fall 1963 races at Mosport, Bridgehampton, Kent, Riverside, and Laguna Seca. Leading in the year-end attendance figures were the Times Grand Prix at Riverside (84,600) and the Monterey Pacific Grand Prix at Laguna Seca (60,000). Dave MacDonald, a virtual unknown in international racing, won both of those prestigious races in a Shelby American King Cobra Cooper-Ford. At Riverside, Jim Hall debuted his radical new rear-engine Chaparral 2, which would change the whole look of professional sports car racing forever.

When the teams traveled to Nassau for the traditional season-ending spectacle, Chevrolet sprang an unexpected and an unwelcome surprise on the Cobras with the debut of the highly modified Corvette Grand Sports and the well-equipped, Chevrolet-backed Mecom and Chaparral teams. By the end of 1963, it was apparent that professional road racing was here to stay.

In 1964 nine races were on the USRRC schedule, and Jim Hall and Dave MacDonald waged a tremendous early-season battle for the Driver's Championship. Sadly, this crowd-pleasing contest was terminated by MacDonald's premature death at Indianapolis in May 1964, and Hall went on to win that championship. Once again, Shelby American won the Manufacturers' Championship.

Once again, several cars that were to figure in the spectacular endurance races of the mid-1960s made themselves known in early 1964. The Daytona Cobra Coupe, Porsche 904, Ferrari GTO Series II, and Ferrari 250LM all made their debut at Daytona in February, and the Ford GT40 first appeared at the LeMans Test Weekend in April.

An undermanned Shelby American team decided to go to Europe and take on Ferrari on the great Italian team's home ground. After an uphill and courageous battle by the American team, Ferrari was able to retain its world championship. But the best was yet to come.

Once again, the lucrative fall pro series drew the cream of the crop of the world's top drivers, teams, and cars. Bruce McLaren showed up at Mosport in September 1964 with the first of the many legendary cars that were to bear his name. Though very fast, the McLaren M1A proved to be fragile. Eventually those problems would be sorted out, and soon the McLaren sports racing car would be at the top of the heap.

The professional races run at Riverside and Laguna Seca again drew record crowds and record entries. At the Times Grand Prix at Riverside, well-known American oval track driver Parnelli Jones won the first

Jack McAfee (88) and Ken Miles (50) put on some of the West Coast's most memorable racing in their rival Porsches at Pomona. This fierce rivalry extended over a number of years, and the racing was always close with no holds barred.

sports car race that he ever competed in. Jones' victory also gave the Shelby American King Cobra its second consecutive win at Riverside. Roger Penske won his second Monterey Grand Prix in three years at Laguna Seca. (His first was in 1962.)

At Nassau, Penske became the only driver ever to win all three of the major races (Tourist Trophy, Governor's Trophy, and Nassau Trophy) in the same year. After Nassau, Penske shocked the racing world by announcing his retirement from competitive driving, to concentrate on his growing business ventures. The racing world, however, was soon to learn it hadn't heard the last of Roger Penske.

Also after Nassau, Ford Motor Company decided to shift the unsuccessful Ford GT40 program from John Wyer to Shelby American. That transfer of cars took place in mid-December, less than eight weeks before the Shelby team was scheduled to run them in the first FIA race of the year at Daytona. It would be a short, busy winter at Shelby's shop in Venice, California.

The September 1962 Canadian Grand Prix for Sports Cars brought together an outstanding international starting field. Waiting on the starting line of the wet Mosport circuit are Jim Hall's Chaparral 1 (4), Roger Penske's Cooper Monaco (6), Dan Gurney's Lotus 19 (96), Francis Bradley's Lotus 19 (25), John Cannon's Dailu-Chevrolet (411), Ludwig Heimrath's Porsche RS 61 (39), and Jo Bonnier's Porsche RS 62 Spyder 8-Cylinder (1).

The 1965 season opened at Daytona on February 24, and it was there that the Ford GT40, driven by Ken Miles and Lloyd Ruby, was able to finish and win its first race. The new Ferrari 330P2 made its debut at Daytona, qualified on the pole, and proved to be very competitive until a broken axle put it out of the race.

In 1965 the organizers of Sebring decided to include sports racing cars in the annual 12-hour race, much to the consternation of the factories that ran prototypes and GT cars. As a result of this decision, Ferrari withdrew all of its official factory entries and, against all odds, Jim Hall and Hap Sharp won the race in their Chaparral 2. The Lola T70, another car that was to have a huge impact on professional sports car racing, made its North American racing debut at Sebring.

The USRRC opened its 10-race season at Pensacola, Florida, in April 1965 with George Follmer winning the Driver's Championship race in his under-two-liter Lotus-Porsche. When the season concluded at Road America in September, Shelby American had taken the Manufacturers' Championship for the third consecutive time, and Follmer had won a rather disputed Driver's Championship over Jim Hall.

The SCCA decided that the Manufacturers' Championship would be terminated after the 1965 season, due to the manufacturers' lack of interest. It is very likely that the withdrawal of the Shelby American–backed Cobra team from USRRC and FIA racing precipitated that decision.

In 1965 the other North American and English Group 7 races were dominated by the Chaparral and the Lola T70. By the end of the year, Chaparral had concluded the greatest season that it would ever have by starting 22 races and winning 16 of them. The Lola T70 was the only car that was capable of seriously challenging the Chaparral in 1965, but, although it won several major races, its fragilities continued to be evident.

The McLaren team tried a new body style for its M1A, but the car remained short of horsepower and was still several years away from its eventual domination. The endurance prototype battle between Ford and Ferrari heated up and, once again, Ferrari came away with that championship in spite of Ford's overwhelming numbers and huge cash expenditures. Ford did unveil two very fast—but fragile—prototype 427-cid Mark IIs at LeMans in June 1965. Those two cars were the fastest ever to run at LeMans up to that time, but gearbox problems put them out of the race while they were well in the lead.

Masten Gregory, in his Lotus 19 (71), takes the lead on the second lap at Mosport. He leads John Cannon (411), Dan Gurney (96), Roger Penske (6), and Ludwig Heimrath (39) early in the race.

Those Fords did, however, signal the company's future intentions for its endurance racing program. Once again Ferrari, as in 1964, had proved to its larger and much richer competitor that you must finish to win and that experience is the best teacher.

It was a different story in the World GT Championship, however, where Shelby American, with its Cobra, became the first American company to win that championship. The fall pro series, including Nassau, was completely dominated by the Chaparral team, with the exception of Mosport, won by John Surtees, and Laguna Seca, won by Walt Hansgen, both driving Lola T70s. The big news at the end of the year was the announcement that the Can-Am series would start in September 1966, replacing the Fall Pro Series that had been so successful over the previous few years.

John Cannon (411), Jack Brabham in a Lotus 23 (9), Roger Penske (6), and Ludwig Heimrath (39). Cannon finished 15th, Penske did not finish ("DNFed"), Brabham finished 4th, and Heimrath finished 5th.

Masten Gregory completed a sweep of the two professional sports car races held at Mosport in 1962 by winning the Canadian Grand Prix in the ex-Stirling Moss UDT-Laystall Lotus 19.

Roy Gane, Roger Penske's chief mechanic, is busy at his Updraught Engineering shop, in 1962, assembling the 2.7-liter Climax engine that would power one of the most controversial cars to ever appear in professional sports car racing.

The first race for the Cooper Zerex Special was at the October 1962 Times Grand Prix. This well-known Riverside race, with its large international race entry, provided a perfect showcase at which to debut this most unusual ex-Formula One car. At first glance, it seemed that this car was a single seat vehicle that placed the driver in the center of the frame. That would constitute an obvious rules violation, since the rule book stated that all sports cars must have a passenger seat and not be a single seater. As soon as the car was unloaded from its trailer, the protests started flying.

With a large crowd of media, mechanics, and drivers watching, Roger Penske calmly unbuttoned a left-side body panel that revealed a rather cramped and small passenger seat. Penske is seen here demonstrating the less-than-desirable legroom provided by the so-called passenger seat. What most of the competitors didn't know at the time was that Penske had brought in the SCCA's chief technical inspector to view the car while it was a work in progress, and the inspector said that the car was completely legal according to the rule book.

If it hadn't been for all of the controversy created by the arrival of the Zerex Special, the biggest and most exciting news of the weekend would have been two of the GT entries that participated in one of the support races, the Three-Hour Endurance Race on the Saturday before the big Sunday race. Four of the brand-new Corvette Z06 Corvette Stingrays were on hand at Riverside for their racing debut. Driven by Doug Hooper (119), Bob Bondurant (614), Jerry Grant, and Dave MacDonald, these cars made their first race a winning one, with Hooper taking the victory. That race, however, had produced another competitor that was even more spectacular than the Corvettes—the Shelby American Cobra.

By 1962, the Times Grand Prix had developed into one of the most anticipated races in the world for drivers and teams alike. After four years of incredible success, it seemed that all of the world's greatest teams and drivers sought an entry into the race. By the time the official entry list was released to the public, it contained a who's who of motor racing. Walt Hansgen in his Cooper-Buick (63) leads the all-star field into Turn 6 at Riverside on the first lap. Roger Penske's Zerex Special (6), Bruce McLaren's Cooper Monaco (5), Jerry Grant's Lotus 19-Buick (8), Jim Hall's Chaparral 1 (66), Masten Gregory's Lotus 19 (3), Lloyd Ruby's Lotus 19 (26), John Cannon's Dailu-Chevrolet (411), and Graham Hill's Cooper Monaco (57) all give chase.

The Shelby American Cobra, driven by the well-known West Coast veteran driver Bill Krause, opened up a huge lead in its debut race, only to have a wheel hub break with victory in sight. The Cobra became the talk of the pits, and the production sports car world was put on notice. The "XP" painted on the side of the Corvettes and the Cobra stood for "Experimental Production," a class created for this race only. This stretch of the rules allowed the as-yet unhomologated Corvette and Cobra to run in this race, because they were obviously production cars. The two cars were just too new to have reached the required 100 units required for homologation.

Chuck Daigh's Maserati Tipo 151 (62), Jack Brabham's Lotus 23 (4), Ken Miles' Maserati Tipo 61 (53), and Pete Lovely's Lotus 23 (94) battle for position early in the race.

A young and relatively unknown John Cannon (411) impressed the record crowd of 76,400 with his driving ability and the speed of his Canadian-built Dailu-Chevrolet. Here, Cannon leads Formula One World Champion Graham Hill's Cooper Monaco into Turn 6. Note the different lines.

One of the highlights of the 1962 season was the wheel-to-wheel battle for the lead that ran for many laps between Dan Gurney in his Lotus 19 (96) and Roger Penske driving the Zerex Special (6). Gurney started at the back of the pack because of mechanical trouble and came through the entire field within the first few laps to challenge Penske for the lead. The two competitors raced this way until Gurney was permanently sidelined by a minor transmission problem, and Penske went on to a record win.

Roger Penske accepts the winner's trophy as Lisa Penske (sitting on the left side of the car) looks on. An amused Dick Van Dyke watches from the far right while Bob Holbert (far left) and Phil Hill (third from left) also look on.

Enough said.

Augie Pabst (left), Walt Hansgen (center), and Briggs Cunningham (right) look intent during an early practice session at Laguna Seca in 1962.

Whenever Augie Pabst and Roger Penske were together at a race, no one ever quite knew what to expect from the two pranksters. At the Pacific Grand Prix, the tow car pulling the entries of Pabst and Penske showed up in the pits sporting a moose head, complete with racing helmet and goggles, that had been "borrowed" from the lobby wall of the Mark Thomas Inn.

One of the wonderful things about photographing the start of any race at Laguna Seca was the great position on the hill that could afford you the chance to get the entire field in the picture as the green flag fell. In the first heat of the 1962 Pacific Grand Prix, Roger Penske's Zerex Special (6) leads Walt Hansgen's Cooper-Buick (63). Also seen are Jim Hall's Chaparral 1 (66), Masten Gregory's Lotus 19 (3), Lloyd Ruby's Lotus 19 (26), Bruce McLaren's Cooper Monaco (5), Dan Gurney's Lotus 19 (96), Graham Hill's Cooper Monaco (57), Alan Connell's Cooper Monaco (55), Tim Mayer's Cooper Monaco (17), and others toward the very fast Turn 1.

Dan Gurney (96) and Lloyd Ruby (26) had the crowd on their feet with their nose-to-tail battle for the lead. Gurney and Ruby ran the entire first heat, often swapping positions, in this manner. Gurney won the heat, while Ruby faded to fourth with brake problems.

Opposite: Innes Ireland, behind the wheel of his Lotus 19 (15), attempts to hold off Jim Hall's Chaparral 1 (66) as they both drop down Laguna Seca's famous corkscrew. Hall finished 5th and Ireland 10th.

Bruce McLaren demonstrates an interesting way to get down the corkscrew.

In the second heat, Roger Penske and Dan Gurney raced this way until Gurney broke a ring and pinion gear. Lloyd Ruby, however, came through the field to win the second heat, but Penske won the race overall, based on his two second-place finishes. Penske became the first driver to win both the Times Grand Prix and the Pacific Grand Prix. on consecutive weekends. Penske also became the last USAC road racing champion, since the USAC dropped the road racing division after the 1962 season.

The one and only Grand Prix of Puerto Rico was run in November 1962, and it attracted a small but competitive field. Awaiting the fall of the green flag are Roger Penske in his Zerex Special (7) and Tim Mayer in his Cooper Monaco (4). Also seen are Rafi Rosales' Elva Mark VI (6), Dan Gurney's Porsche RS 62 8-cylinder (10), Ludwig Heimrath's Porsche RS 61 (39), and Bob Hurt's Ferrari TR60 (36). Penske won the race, with Mayer in second place and Gurney finishing third.

Mechanics from the Rosebud Racing Team make final preparations to the Lotus 19 that Innes Ireland would drive at Nassau. This Lotus could compete with either an under-two-liter engine or an over-two-liter engine, depending on the nature of the race. The Team Rosebud Ferrari GTO is in the background.

A very strong international field started the Nassau Trophy Race for GT cars. Shown here setting off on the pace lap are Ferrari GTOs driven by Innes Ireland (4), Roger Penske (85), and Lorenzo Bandini (21). Also in the running are Marvin Panch's Ford (26), Allan Wylie's Ferrari (81), Charlie Kolb's Ferrari GTO (82), Peter Bethell's Jaguar E-Type (331), and Shelby Cobras driven by John Everly (106) and Bill Krause (98). Penske was the winner of the race in the John Mecom Ferrari GTO.

End of the line for the Dailu-Chevrolet. Driver John Cannon was unhurt.

In February 1963, the United States Road Racing Championship (USRRC) ran its first race at Daytona. A driver's championship was established for the modified cars, while a manufacturers' championship was established for the GT cars. By the time that the third race of the eight-race series was run at Laguna Seca in June 1963, the bugs had been worked out and a large field was present when the weekend began. Bob Holbert (196) and Ken Miles (198) put on a real show in the Manufacturers' Championship, with Holbert taking the first of many USRRC wins for Shelby American.

Ireland wins the Nassau Trophy Race on a very rainy afternoon. This was the third win in a row for the Lotus 19.

Two Ferrari GTOs came to Laguna Seca to try to increase the large points lead that Ferrari maintained over the Cobra at that time. Frank Crane (9) and Ed Cantrell (11), both in GTOs, ran a good race but failed to add any points to the Ferrari total.

Chuck Parsons (10) scored a stunning upset in the Laguna Seca Driver's Championship race by defeating a large field of over-two-liter sports cars with his under-two-liter Lotus 23.

Lloyd Ruby won the first heat of the Player's 200 at Mosport in June 1963. Riding in his J. Frank Harrison Lotus 19 on the victory lap is mechanic Jerry Eisert.

Chuck Daigh, driving the Arciero Lotus 19, was the overall winner of the Player's 200. Daigh had a second-place finish in the first heat and was the winner of the second heat. Ruby did not finish the second heat and Jim Hall finished second overall.

Left: Dave MacDonald (left) and Ole Olsen (right) work to fit a Ford Cobra engine in a Cooper Monaco chassis at the Shelby American shop in Venice, California. These cars would soon become known as King Cobras, and they would dominate the two major professional sports car races at Riverside and Laguna Seca in October 1963.

Opposite, top: Pedro Rodriguez, driving a Genie Mark VIII (448), leads Jerry Grant in his Lotus 19-Buick (8) and Dave Ridenour in his Genie Mark II (146) at the August 1963 USRRC Race at Kent, Washington. Rodriguez won the race, giving him his first USRRC win and the Genie marque its first professional win.

Opposite, bottom: Lance Reventlow won the first race in the front engine Scarab at Santa Barbara in May 1958, while Augie Pabst (seen here) won the car's last race at the August 1963 Continental Divide USRRC race. How many other racing cars do you know that had a winning record for over five years? The front engine Scarab was retired after its final race at the Pacific Grand Prix in October 1963.

The Hansgen/Richards lightweight Jaguar E-Type (61) leads the Pabst/Penske Ferrari GTO (7) at the September 1963 Road America 500 at Elkhart Lake, Wisconsin. This was the type of close racing seen in the USSRC Manufacturers' Races during its first season of competition. Both cars finished the 500-mile race, the Jaguar in 11th place and the Ferrari in 7th place.

Pedro Rodriguez prepares to go out and win the September 1963 Canadian Grand Prix in his North American Racing Team (NART) Ferrari 250P.

There was always a substantial number of GT cars entered in the Canadian Grand Prix. David Piper (3) and Bob Grossman (30), both in Ferrari GTOs, race with the Scarab of Don Divine (24) in the early laps. Devine finished third in the five-year-old Scarab, while both GTOs finished well down in the ranks.

The Bridgehampton 500 FIA GT race saw Dan Gurney (99) win the first of many FIA GT races for the Shelby American Cobra. Surrounding Gurney at the start of the race are the Cobras of Ken Miles (98) and Bob Holbert (97) and the Jaguar E-Types of Walt Hansgen (61) and Briggs Cunningham (60).

Right: The Bridgehampton 500 race was open to all comers, and Walt Hansgen won it in his Cunningham Team Cooper-Buick. Bob Holbert is behind Hansgen, and long-time Cunningham mechanic Alfred Momo is at the far right.

Chapter 2 continues on page 101

Color Gallery

Ricardo Rodriguez, who began racing as a youth in Mexico at age 17, prepares to qualify his Porsche RSK for the October 1959 Los Angeles Times Grand Prix at Riverside.

Augie Pabst (1) and Lance Reventlow (16) drove these two Meister Brauser Scarabs at the April 1960 Los Angeles Examiner Grand Prix at Riverside. Reventlow practiced his car but did not attempt to qualify, and Pabst did not finish the race due to engine failure.

Carroll Shelby, driving the Camoradi USA Maserati Tipo 61, won the final race of his driving career at the Los Angeles Examiner Grand Prix in April 1960.

Stirling Moss drove one of the two Lotus 19 Monte Carlos (Dan Gurney had the other) in the United States at the October 1960 Los Angeles Times Grand Prix at Riverside. Moss led the race until the 10th lap, when he went out of the race with clutch and transmission problems.

Bill Krause upset a world-class field when he won the October 1960 Los Angeles Times Grand Prix at Riverside. He used his winnings to establish a Honda dealership, and he became a very successful businessman.

In October 1961 the UDT-Laystall team returned to the West Coast Fall Series, entering two Lotus 19s in the Times Grand Prix. Stirling Moss drove Number 7 and led for 27 laps until he had to pit with transmission problems. He rejoined the race but finished in 16th place, seven laps off of the pace. Olivier Gendebien drove Number 9 in the under-two-liter class and finished 7th overall and 1st in class.

Roger Penske's Cooper-Zerex Special (6) and Walt Hansgen's Cooper-Buick (63) lead Bruce McLaren's Cooper (5), Jerry Grant's Lotus 19-Buick (8), Jim Hall's Chaparral 1 (66), the Lotus 19s of Masten Gregory (3) and Lloyd Ruby (26), and the rest of a strong international starting field out of Turn 1 on the first lap of the 1962 Los Angeles Times Grand Prix. Penske went on to win the race.

The Masten Gregory Lotus 19 (3) and Jim Hall Chaparral 1 (66) approach the top of Laguna Seca's famous Corkscrew during the October 1962 Pacific Grand Prix.

Opposite: Roger Penske adjusts the mirror on his Cooper Zerex Special as he sits on the starting grid prior to the start of the November 1962 Puerto Rican Grand Prix. He won the race.

The well-prepared John Mecom Ferrari GTO, with Roger Penske and Augie Pabst driving, finished fourth overall and first in GT at Sebring in March 1963.

By the day of the October 1963 Los Angeles Times Grand Prix, the controversial configuration of the Zerex Special had been altered to include the second seat that the rules of the day required. John Mecom had become the owner of the car, but Roger Penske was still the driver, and he finished second overall behind Dave MacDonald in the big race.

Graham Hill drove a Lotus 23B in the 1963 Times Grand Prix and finished 10th overall.

Awaiting the start of a practice session at the June 1965 Player's 200 are Jim Hall's Chaparral 2 (66), Hugh P. K. Dibley's Lola T70 (5), Ludwig Heimrath's McLaren M1A (1), Walt McKay's Cooper-Ford (93), Bob Johnson's Shelby Cobra (33), Chuck Dietrich's Elva BMW (57), Gary Gove's Cheetah-Chevrolet (17), Joe Buzzetta's Elva Porsche (3), Wayne Kelly's Porsche Special (81), and Bob Slotemaker's Porsche 904 (10).

A. J. Foyt literally drove the wheels off of the Scarab that he raced very successfully in several competitions in 1963 and 1964. While running second at the June 1964 Players 200, he lost a wheel shortly before the race ended.

Jerry Grant, racing a Lotus 19-Chevrolet (8), leads Charlie Hayes in a Lang Cooper-Chevrolet (97) and Jim Hall in a Chaparral 2 (66) out of Moss Corner during the Player's 200 in June 1965. Hall finished second and Hayes sixth; Grant did not finish.

When the Chaparral 2D arrived at Daytona in February 1966, it looked like a Chaparral 2 with a top, which, in fact, it was. No one knew what to expect, because the car had just been completed the week before the race, and it had never been tested. Phil Hill and Jo Bonnier put the new Chaparral on the front row and led the first seven laps before succumbing to the numerous teething problems associated with any new, untested race car. Jim Hall, Jo Bonnier, Troy Rogers, and Franz Weis gather around as Phil Hill (seated in car) gives his impressions of the car following a Daytona practice session. Note the 2C-type flipper on the rear deck. That experiment didn't work as well as was hoped, and it was removed permanently following the Daytona race.

Jimmy Clark drove his Lotus 30-Ford with typical bravado at the 1965 Player's 200. As was the case in most races in which he drove the Lotus 30 during its brief racing career, Clark was bedeviled by engine and suspension gremlins.

Denis Hulme (81), Dan Gurney (30), and Mark Donohue (6), all driving Lola T70s, contend for the lead at the September 1966 Mosport Can-Am. Donohue was the winner.

Responding to the fall of the green flag at the April 1967 USRRC at Riverside are Peter Revson (52), Lothar Motschenbacher (11), Bob Bondurant (51), Skip Scott (91), Bud Morley (71), and Chuck Parsons (10), all driving McLaren M1Bs, and Jerry Grant (78) and Mike Goth (4) in Lola T70s. The winner (not shown) was Mark Donohue, driving a Sunoco Lola T70.

Right: The new Ferrari 312P driven by Chris Amon and Mario Andretti was in a strong position to win the March 1969 Sebring race, but an overheating problem and later a miscalculation of fuel consumption cost them a chance to win in their first time out with that car.

The first turbocharged car that appeared in the Can-Am series was the McKee, powered by a twin-turbocharged Oldsmobile engine. USAC Champion Joe Leonard drove the car at the June 1969 St. Jovite race and finished eighth. The McKee Team ran into technical and financial difficulty and was forced to withdraw at midseason.

The Howmet TX Turbocar (76) built by McKee Engineering was one of the most fascinating cars to appear at Daytona in February 1968. Driven by Ray Heppenstall, Dick Thompson, and Ed Lowther, the car was powered by a Continental gas turbine that produced approximately 325 brake horsepower. The Turbocar showed great potential before it was put out of contention by brake problems. The best finish for this car was a third place at Watkins Glen. Here, the Howmet car laps the Robson/Rogers E Type Jaguar (42) as they leave the infield and approach the Daytona banking.

With less than an hour remaining in the 1970 Sebring race, Mario Andretti was put into the third-place Ignacio Giunti/Nino Vaccarella Ferrari 512S with the express instructions to make every attempt to win. He drove the car to a spectacular come-from-behind win over the Steve McQueen/Peter Revson Porsche 908.

Above: The all-conquering McLaren M8Bs sit on the starting grid at the beautiful Edmonton International Speedway in the July 1969 Can-Am.

Inset: The racing debut of the 6.2-liter, 640-plus-brake horsepower Ferrari 612P was at Watkins Glen in July 1969. Chris Amon demonstrated the car's fantastic potential, but continuous engine problems and lack of proper factory support derailed the project. Maybe the Ferrari 612P didn't live up to its potential, but the sound of it sure did.

Left: Jackie Oliver and Pedro Rodriguez drove this battle-damaged Porsche 917 to a fourth place overall at the 1971 Sebring 12-Hour. The vehicle sustained the damage in a highly volatile collision with the Donohue/Hobbs Sunoco Ferrari 512M. The accident nearly resulted in a fist fight between Donohue and Rodriguez.

Dan Gurney accepts his first of two consecutive Can-Am win medals at Mosport in June 1970. He also won at St. Jovite two weeks later.

Top right: Bob Bondurant's McLaren M8D (12) leads Mark Donohue's Ferrari 512M (6) and Peter Revson's McLaren M8F (7) at Watkins Glen in July 1971. Revson won, while Bondurant finished 16th and Donohue failed to finish.

Center right: Watkins Glen was a unique Can-Am race because it invited the drivers of the surviving endurance cars from the previous day's 6-hour race to participate if they chose. Richard Attwood's Porsche 917K (91) leads Cliff Apel's McLaren M6B (37) and Derek Bell's Porsche 917K (93) at this event. Attwood finished 13th, Bell finished 11th, and Apel did not finish.

Mario Andretti debuted a newly designed Ferrari 712M powered by a specially built seven-liter engine at Watkins Glen in 1971. Andretti finished fourth overall, but the car was withdrawn from the series after this race for unknown reasons.

Can-Am Series Champion Peter Revson, driving a McLaren M8F (7), and Jackie Stewart, in a Lola T260 (1), enter Riverside's famous Turn 6 during the early part of the 1971 Times Grand Prix.

At Donnybrooke, Francois Cevert, racing a McLaren M8F (22), was the last person to win a Can-Am race in a McLaren in 1972. Mark Donohue and George Follmer won the rest of the races in their Porsche 917/10K. Here, Cevert leads David Hobbs' Lola T310 (1) and Lothar Motschenbacher's McLaren M8D (11) on his way to a third place overall.

Denis Hulme's McLaren M20 (5) and Mark Donohue's Porsche 917/10K (6) lead a large field of cars into Turn 7 during the October 1972 Times Grand Prix. Hulme's lead was short-lived, and he blew an engine on the 45th lap.

The Beltoise/Cevert/Pescarolo Matra MS670 (3) was the class of the field at the 1973 Daytona 24 Race. As often happens in endurance racing, problems plagued the Matra; the car was enjoying an 11-lap lead over the nearest competitor when a connecting rod broke in the engine.

Peter Gregg and Hurley Haywood, racing their brand-new Porsche Carrera RS (59), were the surprise winners at Daytona in 1973.

The Henri Pescarolo/Gerald Larrousse Matra MS670 (33) leads the Arturo Merzario/Carlos Pace Ferrari 312PB (11) in a race for the lead at the 1973 Watkins Glen 6-Hour race. The Matra won and the Ferrari finished third.

The Penske crew prepare to push Mark Donohue away during practice for the July 1973 Watkins Glen Can-Am.

You can almost hear all of that incredible noise! Racing two and three abreast up the Laguna Seca front straight in October 1973 are Mark Donohue's Porsche 917/30 (6), David Seville-Peck's Costello SP7 (45), Vic Elford's Shadow DN2 Turbo (102), John Cannon's McLaren M20 (98), Mario Andretti's McLaren M20 (96), Charlie Kemp's Porsche 917/10 (23), David Hobbs' McLaren M20 (73), Ed Felter's McLaren M8E (47), and Jody Scheckter's Porsche 917/10 (0).

George Follmer, racing a Porsche 917/10K (16), won the Road Atlanta Can-Am in July 1973 but didn't win again that year. He finished second to Donohue in the overall series points. As seen here, early in the race at Laguna Seca, Follmer leads Jackie Oliver in a Shadow DN2 (101) and Hurley Haywood in a Porsche 917/10 (59) down the corkscrew. Follmer did not finish, but Oliver finished second and Haywood came in third.

In 1973, Mark Donohue won the race at Laguna Seca and the series championship. He would become the last American to win the Can-Am championship.

In the Can-Am series in 1974, Jackie Oliver, driving a Shadow DN4 (101), won four of the five races and the series championship.

The final race of the Can-Am, as we knew it, was at Road America in August 1974, and that race was won by Scooter Patrick in a McLaren M20 (8). A very special era of sports car racing died the day the Can-Am ended.

A one-hour endurance race was run on the Sunday morning prior to the start of the 1963 Times Grand Prix, and the Cobras dominated that race by sweeping the first four places. Bob Bondurant (99) was the winner, with Dan Gurney (97) finishing third and Lew Spencer (98) finishing fourth. Allen Grant (not in the picture) finished second. Part of the record crowd of 82,600 can be seen behind the three Shelby team Cobras as they crest the hill at Riverside's Turn 7.

Dave Ridenour in his Genie Mark VIII (146) passes Frank Gardner's Brabham BT8 (25) as the two cars exit Turn 6. This was typical of the exciting action that occurred when this many great drivers were on the same track at the same time.

Dave MacDonald receives a pit signal from his boss, Carroll Shelby, during his record-setting drive to victory at the 1963 Times Grand Prix. MacDonald lapped the entire world-class field that day and broke every record in the book in what many of us thought was one of the greatest races of his life.

When the green flag fell for the start of the Times Grand Prix, Jim Hall (5), driving his radical new Chaparral 2, shot into the lead and ran at a record-setting pace until the car was forced out of the race by electrical failure. Almost every top racing driver in the world was in the starting field for this race. Jim Clark, John Surtees, Dan Gurney, A. J. Foyt, Roger Penske, Roy Salvadori, Lloyd Ruby, Frank Gardner, Pedro Rodriguez, Walt Hansgen, Ken Miles, Bob Holbert, and Graham Hill were all there. No wonder the crowds got bigger every year.

Right: When the three newly modified Corvette Grand Sports arrived in Nassau in December 1963, their appearance shocked everyone who saw them. Carroll Shelby (right) and Ken Miles (second from right) try to question a tight-lipped Roger Penske (light shirt) about the car's potential, but no direct answers were forthcoming.

Opposite, top: Jim Clark made his first of several West Coast racing appearances in the fall of 1963. At Laguna Seca during his only racing appearance there, Clark drove the well-known Arciero Lotus 19 and led the race until mechanical problems forced him to retire.

Opposite, bottom left: Bob Holbert's King Cobra (99) heads up the field on the way to Turn 1. Behind Holbert, Walt Hansgen's Genie-Ford (61), Lloyd Ruby's Harrison Special (3), Jim Clark's Lotus 19 (5), Jim Hall's Chaparral 2 (66), A. J. Foyt's Scarab (91), Pedro Rodriguez's Genie-Ford (66), Roger Penske's Mecom Special (17), Tim Mayer's Lotus 23B (11), and Graham Hill's Lotus 23B (1) give chase. Barely visible in 17th place is Dave MacDonald.

Opposite, bottom right: Dave MacDonald, driving his King Cobra (98), leads Dick Thompson's Maserati Tipo 64 (62), Graham Hill's Lotus 23B (1), and Rodger Ward's Cooper-Chevrolet (111) down the corkscrew. MacDonald, in spite of a bent frame and a faulty transmission, came charging through the field to win the race. This was the first time that the Pacific Grand Prix was run from start to finish in one heat.

Augie Pabst in his Lola-Chevrolet (00) pulls away from the Corvette Grand Sports of Jim Hall (80) and Dick Thompson (65) to win the Nassau Tourist Trophy.

A. J. Foyt was the winner of the Governor's Trophy and the Nassau Trophy in the John Mecom–owned Scarab Chevrolet. A jubilant John and Katsie Mecom stand at the right side of the picture. The 1963 Nassau Speed Week was an overpowering victory for the Mecom-Chevrolet team since they had soundly defeated the highly touted Ford-powered cars of Shelby American.

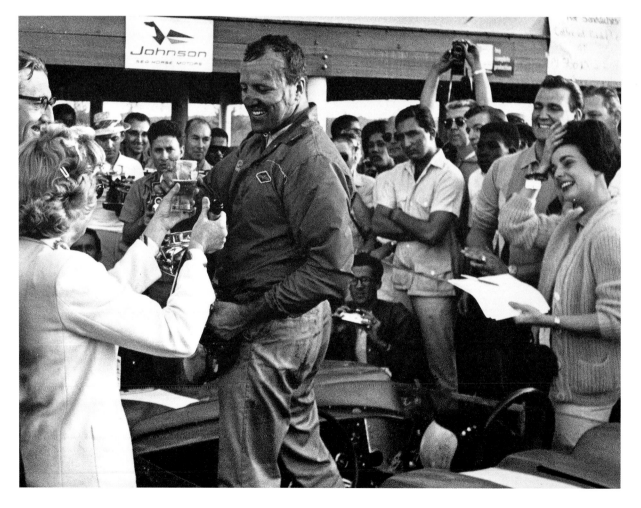

The first major race to be run for sports cars in 1964 was the American Challenge Cup in February at Daytona. This race was open to all prototypes, modified sports cars, and GT cars. One of the most interesting entrants was the Ferrari 250LM entered by the North American Racing Team and driven by Pedro Rodriguez. Although the Ferrari performed reasonably well in its first outing, it did not finish, due to a minor engine problem.

One of the finest races ever run was seen by virtually no one. (Note the empty grandstands in the photo.) During the American Challenge Cup race, Dan Gurney, driving a Lotus 19-Ford (21), and A. J. Foyt, with a Mecom Scarab-Chevrolet (35), raced wheel-to-wheel and exchanged the lead numerous times until Gurney fell victim to a faulty transmission late in the race. Foyt went on to his final win in the Scarab.

One of the most spectacular ways to get your car seen by the world media in the mid-1960s was to exhibit at the New York Auto Show. Note Ford's new "Total Performance" concept.

In 1964 the Shelby American Cobra completely dominated the USRRC Manufacturers' Championship, which it won for the second time. Ed Leslie (98) and Ken Miles (50) completely ran away from a very strong field at Laguna Seca in May.

Below: Bob Holbert in his King Cobra (114), first off the line at the start of the USRRC Driver's Championship race, is followed by Jim Hall's Chaparral 2 (366), Skip Hudson's Cooper-Chevrolet (9), Roger Penske's Chaparral 2 (367), Chuck Daigh's Lotus 19 (5), Dave Ridenour's Genie-Buick (146), John Cannon's Scarab (8), Ed Leslie's Cobra (98), and Dave MacDonald's Lang Cooper-Ford (97). Hall won the race in the first outing for a Chaparral equipped with an automatic transmission.

While in a close contest for the lead, A. J. Foyt's Scarab (8) and Bruce McLaren's Cooper-Oldsmobile (47) lap Allen Grant's Cheetah (8) at the Player's 200 at Mosport in June 1964. The race between Foyt and McLaren was close and spectacular until Foyt went out with mechanical problems.

Opposite: The early part of the USSRC season provided some very exciting and extremely close racing between Dave MacDonald in a King Cobra and Jim Hall in a Chaparral 2. By the time the USRRC series moved to Kent, Washington, in May 1964, MacDonald had a slim lead over Hall in the Driver's Championship, and his narrow win there increased his lead. On the victory lap, MacDonald (helmet) took his friend and competitor Hall (with flag) along for the ride. The race was bittersweet, however, because MacDonald was killed days later at Indianapolis.

Bruce McLaren takes his crew chief and good friend Tyler Alexander for a victory lap ride after winning both heats and the overall at the Player's 200. Bruce McLaren had purchased the ex-Penske Zerex Special from John Mecom and had installed an aluminum Oldsmobile engine in it. After several successful outings in England, McLaren brought the car to North America to compete with success against a quality field at the Canadian race.

No, folks, it's not a Mobile Oil commercial, it's just the official refueling station for the July 1964 Pikes Peak Hill Climb. Bobby Unser drove this highly modified Arciero Lotus 23 to the sports car championship, utilizing the 2.7-liter engine that normally powered Arciero's Lotus 19.

The Chaparral (68) and the Ferrari 250LM (2) driven by Walt Hansgen and Augie Pabst ran first and second for many laps of the Road America 500, before the Chaparral broke and the Ferrari went on to victory.

The Hall/Penske Corvette Grand Sport was a last-minute entry at the September 1964 Road America 500 because the second Chaparral was not ready. The Grand Sport was driven by Jim Hall, Roger Penske, and Hap Sharp, who also alternated the driving chores in the lone Chaparral entry. After running well in the early part of the race, the Grand Sport suffered from various mechanical malfunctions but was still able to finish third overall.

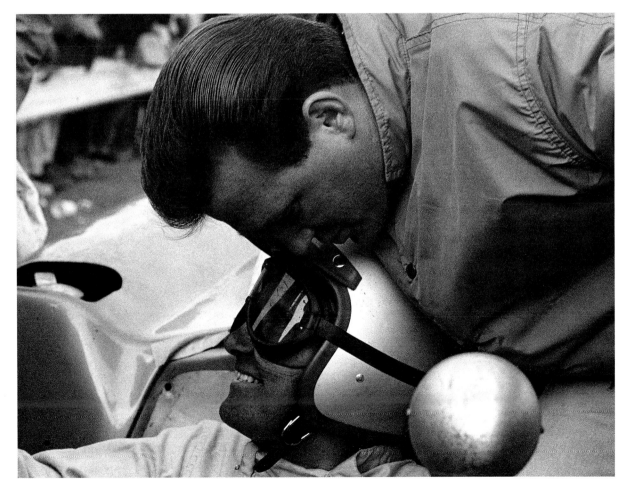

Walt Hansgen and team owner John Mecom celebrate the overall win of the Scarab at the Bridgehampton 500 in September 1964.

Colin Chapman (center) supervises engine adjustments on the Lotus 30 that Jim Clark (background) would drive in the Canadian Sports Car Grand Prix. Clark's race only lasted 15 laps before overheating put the car on the side line.

Below: The Mosport race always had an interesting field of entries because the race was strongly supported by GT cars, and they were allowed to run with the big boys in the big race. Here, Bob Grossman's Ferrari 250 LM (30) chases down the Brabham BT8 of Robert Lamplough (21). Grossman had a 7th place finish, while Lamplough finished 15th.

Jim Clark does a spark plug check on his Lotus 30 at the Times Grand Prix in October 1964.

Below: In 1964 the Corvette Grand Sport roadster was unveiled in Detroit, but it never turned a wheel on the race track until March 1966. Unfortunately by that time, the car was hopelessly outdated and it had very little success in the few races in which it appeared.

Clark's answer to the 1964 "Dan Gurney For President" campaign.

In 1964, Parnelli Jones won the Times Grand Prix on his first attempt. Jones, driving a Shelby American King Cobra (94), leads teammate and seventh-place finisher Richie Ginther (92) out of Turn 7. Jones, one of the most versatile racing stars of that era, was driving the first sports car race of his career.

Opposite: As always, Dan Gurney's luck at the one race that he really wanted to win was dismal. While running at the front of the qualifying race, Gurney's engine blew, forcing him to run the consolation race, which he won. Starting in 31st position, Gurney moved quickly up to 6th before suspension failure put him out of the race. Gurney's Lotus 19-Ford (19) leads Bob Bondurant's King Cobra (93) and Bobby Unser's Lotus 19-Chevrolet (96) through Riverside's very fast Turn 1. Bondurant finished fifth overall, while Unser finished just behind him in sixth place.

Bruce McLaren (left) looks for gremlins under his new car as he and his crew prepare for the October 1964 Pacific Grand Prix. The McLaren was powered by a Traco aluminum Oldsmobile engine.

Dan Gurney (dark jacket) and crew chief Bill Fowler (white shirt) hope their luck will improve at Laguna Seca. It did, as Gurney finished second to Roger Penske's Chaparral in the overall results.

John Mecom (left) pushes his Hussein 1, powered by a seven-liter Chrysler engine off of the boat at the beginning of the December 1964 Nassau Speed Weeks. This car was a real handful, and only A. J. Foyt was brave enough to drive it flat out.

By the time the Ford GT40s arrived at Daytona in 1965, they had undergone a complete face-lift. After working day and night for two months, the Shelby American team fielded two cars that at last proved the potential of the Ford program by qualifying second and third in a strong field of 43 cars that included prototypes, GT cars, and sports racing cars. The Ken Miles/Lloyd Ruby Ford GT40 (73) was never out of the top three positions except for brief, scheduled pit stops. When Gurney (44) went out of the race, the GT40 took the lead and won the 12-hour race in record time. This was the first overall win for the Ford GT40.

Left: Dan Gurney ponders the chances of his Lotus 19-Ford team at Daytona in February 1965. Gurney and codriver Jerry Grant led the race, at record pace, until his car was permanently sidelined on lap 213 with a broken piston.

Opposite: By the end of 1964, Ford Motor Company had grown tired of the unsuccessful racing program being conducted by Ford Advanced Vehicles. The disappointing outing at Nassau was the straw that broke the camel's back, and in mid-December Ford transferred the GT40 racing program to Shelby American. With the new season starting at Daytona in February 1965, no time could be wasted in finding a winning combination for that 2,000-kilometer race. The first test (seen here with Ken Miles driving) was run several days after the first car arrived at the Venice shop. Miles' reaction to the whole thing was, "Bloody awful." The Shelby American team would have its hands full for the next eight weeks.

Hoping to increase spectator attendance, the organizers of the Sebring race decided to allow open-classification sports cars to compete in the 12-hour event in 1965. This change in the rules caused the prompt withdrawal of both the Ferrari and Porsche factory teams because they knew that they had almost no chance for an overall win if the modified sports cars lasted for the entire 12 hours. At the last minute, one factory eight-cylinder Porsche 904 and a number of Ferraris, in various private team colors, showed up. When the race started, the two Chaparral entries (Number 3 and Number 4) with Jim Hall, Hap Sharp, Ronnie Hissom, and Bruce Jennings driving were in the first two starting positions after setting a new qualifying record. Behind the Chaparrals were Ken Miles' Ford GT40 (11), Richie Ginther's Ford GT40 (10), Dan Gurney's Lotus 19-Ford (23), John Cannon's Lola T70 (22), and Pedro Rodriguez's Ferrari 275P (30).

Opposite, top: The McLaren/Miles Ford GT40 (11) laps the Triumph Spitfire (66) of Bob Tullius and Charlie Gates. The Ford went on to finish 2nd overall and 1st in the prototype class, while the Triumph finished 30th overall and 3rd in class.

Opposite, below: The Johnson/Payne Daytona Cobra Coupe (14) is about to be lapped by the Gurney/Grant Lotus 19-Ford (23). This coupe finished seventh overall and second in its GT class, while a similar Cobra Coupe finished fourth overall and won the GT class. In 1965, Shelby American became the only American company to ever win the FIA World Manufacturers' GT Championship. This happened in only the company's third year of competition.

The USRRC Manufacturers' Championship ceased to exist after the completion of the 1965 season due to lack of interest, and, I suspect, the Shelby American domination of the three years that the championship was in existence. The May 1965 Laguna Seca USRRC Manufacturers' race drew the largest field of the year, and it also proved to be the final USRRC race for the official Shelby American team. Jim Hall, driving a Chaparral 2 (66), was the first off of the starting line at Laguna Seca in June 1965 and, after a furious race with Walt Hansgen in a Lola T70 (11) and Don Wester in a Genie-Ford (60), went on to take the win. Behind Hall, Hansgen, and Wester are Dave Ridenour's Genie-Comet (14), Charley Hayes' Lang Cooper-Chevrolet (97), Jerry Titus' Webster-Climax (76), Tony Settember's Lotus 23B (66), George Follmer's Lotus 23B-Porsche (16), and Miles Gupton's Platypus-Porsche (75).

A young and relatively unknown Jackie Stewart made his North American racing debut at Laguna Seca in a factory-sponsored Lotus Cortina. Stewart's debut was not especially spectacular, with a 13th overall finish.

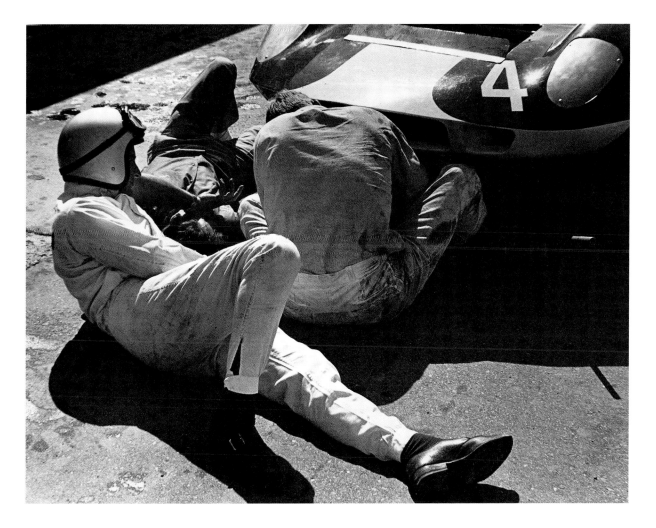

Bruce McLaren relaxes in the foreground as Tyler Alexander works his magic on the team McLaren M1A that was entered in the 1965 Player's 200 at Mosport. McLaren was one of the race leaders before transmission failure forced him to quit.

Three of the legends of the 1960s sports car era are in the same corner at the same time. Jim Hall's Chaparral 2 (66), John Surtees' Lola T70 (11), and Jim Clark's Lotus 30 (82) battle for the lead at the Player's 200. Surtees won the race, with Hall finishing second. Clark failed to finish due to engine problems.

When the green flag fell on the 1965 Canadian Grand Prix, Bruce McLaren, behind the wheel of his McLaren M1A (14) took the lead from David Hobbs' Lola T70 (3), Pedro Rodriguez's Ferrari 365P2 (10), Chris Amon's Ford GTX (15), and Charlie Hayes' McLaren M1A (97). Jim Hall, starting in 18th position, came through the entire field to nip McLaren at the finish line and win the race.

Bruce McLaren checks his Firestone tire temperature report before climbing out of the cockpit of his Team McLaren M1A, after taking the pole position for the Canadian Grand Prix for Sports Cars.

Old pro Dan Gurney (left) gives a young Mario Andretti (right) some advice about driving a sports car at Riverside. The 1965 Times Grand Prix was Andretti's first appearance in a professional sports car race. Unfortunately, his factory Lola T70 was not up to the occasion, and he did not qualify.

Hugh P. K. Dibley, driving a Lola T70 (69), leads Chris Amon (71) into Riverside's Turn 7. Dibley went on to finish seventh overall, while Amon gave the overweight Ford GTX its best finish ever, with a fifth overall.

Sign seen during the 1965 Times Grand Prix.

George Follmer's Lotus 23B-Porsche (16) leads Richard Mecon's McLaren M1A (9) and Mike Goth's McLaren M1A (58) into Turn 9. Follmer had just become the first under-two-liter car to ever win the USRRC Driver's Championship in 1965. But his luck didn't hold at Laguna Seca, and his battered Lotus-Porsche finished well down the chart.

Opposite: When the professional sports car season moved to Laguna Seca in October 1965, all of the European teams boycotted the race because of a dispute over starting money. That fact, however, did not prevent the event from becoming the best, closest, and most exciting race of the 1965 season. Early in the race, Walt Hansgen in his Lola T70 (17) and eventual third-place finisher Don Wester, driving his Genie (60), race for the lead.

Walt Hansgen accepts the winner's plaudits. Hansgen, running most of the race on seven cylinders, held off a hard-charging Hap Sharp for a narrow victory.

Hap Sharp wins the 1965 Times Grand Prix in his Chaparral 2. The Chaparral team had a banner year by winning 16 of the 22 races that the team entered that season.

Right: Whatever the mechanic signaling Parnelli Jones was saying, it must have worked, as Parnelli qualified his Mecom Lola T70 in second place for the November 1965 Las Vegas Grand Prix.

Opposite: At Las Vegas, Jim Hall (65) and Hap Sharp (66) exchanged cars, and Sharp went on to win while Hall, who had to make a gas stop on his next-to-last lap, finished third.

Bob Bondurant in his Lola T70 (111) and Hap Sharp, driving his Chaparral 2 (65), race for the lead during the Nassau Trophy Race. Sharp won and Bondurant finished eighth. After this race, Sharp, who had won three major professional races in a row, decided to retire from the cockpit and move on to team management. He would, however, return occasionally to drive again over the next two years.

Opposite, top: A. J. Foyt (2) put on a wheel-lifting show at Nassau in his 427-cid Ford-powered Lotus 40. Unfortunately, Foyt was only able to complete a total of 17 laps in the two races in which he was entered due to engine problems.

Opposite, bottom: John (Buck) Fulp's Lola T70 (26) leads Charlie Hayes' McLaren M1A (97) and Chris Amon's Ford GTX (4) during the early stages of the Nassau Governor's Trophy race in 1965. Fulp and Hayes dropped out with engine problems, and Amon went on to finish 17th.

The Golden Years

The 1966 season was an accurate forecast of the many exciting things that were to happen in the very near future. Ford started things off with a bang when its newly redesigned 427-cid-powered Mark II swept the first three places at the first running of the 24 Hours of Daytona. Ford also won at Sebring and capped a banner year by finally winning the 24 Hours of LeMans with its second three-car sweep of the season.

By 1966, the USRRC was beginning to lose much of its luster, because many of the series' top names were also participating in factory-backed teams in USAC, NASCAR, and endurance racing. This expanded and varied racing schedule caused numerous scheduling conflicts, and the USRRC lost out to its larger competitors and their higher prize money structure. Chuck Parsons won the USRRC championship in 1966 while driving both a McLaren and Genie.

In 1966 the Can-Am series opened its first season of racing, with John Surtees winning the first event at St. Jovite, Canada, in September. Surtees became the first series champion by winning three of the six races. The Lola T70 was victorious in five of the six races in the series. Chaparral was the winner of the only event that the Lola did not win—Laguna Seca—and that race would be the only one that Jim Hall's legendary cars would win during their five-year (1966-1970) participation in the series.

Ferrari started the 1967 season with a shocking sweep of the first three places at the 24 Hours of Daytona. Ford, still gloating over its 1966 world championship, got caught with its pants down and the

Another important first also occurred at Daytona. The one Corvette entry owned by Roger Penske Racing was seen for the first time. Dick Guldstrand, George Wintersteen, and Ben Moore drove the car to the GT win and 12th overall. This was the first win for Roger Penske as a team owner, and it wasn't long before Penske Racing, with its Sunoco blue sports racing cars, was among the world's best and most popular racing teams. The Miles/Ruby Ford Mark II (98) laps the Penske Racing Corvette on the high banks of Daytona.

The 1966 season got off to a flying start with the all-new 427-cid Ford Mark II and the new Chaparral 2D making their racing debuts at the first running of the 24 Hours of Daytona. The Jo Bonnier/Phil Hill Chaparral 2D (65) and the Ken Miles/Lloyd Ruby Ford Mark II (98) run together around the fourth turn backing followed by the Walt Hansgen/Mark Donohue Ford Mark II, the Mario Andretti/Pedro Rodriguez Ferrari 365P2 (21), and the Dan Gurney/Jerry Grant Ford Mark II (97). Miles and Ruby won the race and led a Ford sweep of the first three places.

At Sebring, Dan Gurney, driving a Ford Mark II (2), was the first to his car at the start, and he led the race until his engine blew in the last turn on the final lap. Behind Gurney are the Mike Parkes Ferrari 330P3 (27), Walt Hansgen Ford Mark II (3), Graham Hill Ford GT40 (24), Ken Miles Ford X1 Roadster (1), and Hap Sharp Chaparral 2D (11). Ken Miles and Lloyd Ruby were, once again, the race winners.

Ford transmissions broken at Daytona. The Dearborn giant woke up by the time of the Sebring race, however, and won that competition with the all-new Mark IV. (That racer, in the company's final race ever in June of that year, won at LeMans for a second time with American drivers Dan Gurney and A. J. Foyt at the wheel. This was the final race at LeMans for the unlimited displacement prototype cars, due to a change in the FIA regulations for the 1968 season.)

Mark Donohue dominated the USRRC championship with his Roger Penske-owned, Sunoco-sponsored Lola T70 by winning five of the six races on the 1967 season's calendar. That year the McLaren team began its five-year domination of the Can-Am series by winning five of the six scheduled races.

The 1968 professional racing season started with Porsche winning the 24 Hours of Daytona, the first of many endurance races it would win. For the third time in three years at Daytona, the winning marque swept the first three spots. Porsche also won Sebring.

Ford did not compete in 1968, since the FIA rule change forbade the company to use the equipment and big-engine technology that it had developed over a three-year period. John Wyer and Gulf Oil formed the Gulf Ford racing team, which capitalized on the small block Ford GT40 that had been developed between 1963 and 1965. This team won LeMans and several other endurance races that season, as well as the FIA Manufacturers' Championship—a considerable achievement, considering the outdated equipment with which it was competing that year.

By 1968, the USRRC was suffering from an extreme lack of interest, because many of its star drivers were also competing in other, more lucrative, professional series. Mark Donohue repeated as USRRC champion in that series' final season of competition; driving the same McLaren M6A with which Bruce McLaren had won the 1967 Can-Am, Donohue won five out of six races. Denis Hulme won the 1968 Can-Am championship by winning three of the six races, while the McLaren marque won all six races.

Porsche turned up the heat in the FIA Manufacturers' Championship in 1969 by winning its first world championship. David Piper and Frank Gardner drove the soon-to-be-legendary Porsche 917, which had made a rather obscure debut at the Nurburgring in May 1969, to a ninth place overall in spite of some serious handling problems. The Gulf Ford team won at LeMans once again and also at Sebring.

Lola scored a shocking win at Daytona with its T70 coupe by beating off a large field of far superior cars, proving that the last man standing would win the race. The McLaren team won all 11 of the Can-Am races in 1969, with Bruce McLaren winning the overall championship. The Porsche factory debuted its first Can-Am car, the 917 PA, in 1969 and used the season as a testing period for both engine and chassis development for the coming endurance season. Too, Ferrari introduced a spectacular six-liter Can-Am car that year. Although the car emitted an unforgettable sound, the Ferrari team could not overcome the continued engine and chassis problems that plagued the car throughout the entire season.

When Penske Racing went to Sebring in March 1966, it took a Corvette Grand Sport roadster as a second entry, along with the Corvette that it had run successfully at Daytona. Although the Corvette Grand Sport had been seen at various East Coast car shows since 1964, it had never been run in competition. Dick Guldstrand and Dick Thompson drove the roadster (10) at Sebring and, although it was very fast in a straight line, it was hopelessly outdated by the numerous midengine cars that had been entered in the race that year. Three and a half hours into the 12-hour race, Thompson went off the road and put a hole in the oil pan of the 427-cid Chevrolet engine. That finished the car's only race as a Penske entry. Behind Thompson, the Shelby Cobra 427 (7) of John Bentley, H. Byrne, and Arthur Latta, and the ill-fated Comstock Ford GT40 (18) of Bob McLean and Jean Oulette give chase. The Cobra finished 22nd overall, and the Ford GT40 crashed, with McLean being fatally injured.

A good field of modified cars appeared on the grid at the USRRC race at Laguna Seca in May 1966. Leading the pack off the line are Mark Donohue's Lola T70 (6), Lothar Motschenbacher's McLaren M1A (27), and John Cannon's Genie-Chevrolet (62). Giving chase are Jerry Hansen's Lotus 19-Chevrolet (44), Ronnie Bucknum's Lola T70 (51), Stan Burnett's Burnett Mark II (61), Ken Miles' Porsche 906 (33), Scooter Patrick's Porsche 906 (32), and Charlie Hayes' McLaren M1A (97). Charlie Hayes was the race winner.

For the 1966 season, the McLaren team had Chris Amon (2) and Bruce McLaren (4) driving its cars. At the Player's 200, Amon and McLaren were on the front row of the grid, with Charlie Hayes' McLaren M1A (97), Jerry Grant's Lola T70 (8), Lothar Motschenbacher's McLaren M1A (11), and John Cannon's Genie-Chevrolet (62) behind the leaders.

In 1966 the McLaren team cars were still powered by the aluminum small block Traco Oldsmobile engine that they had used since 1964. Although very fast, the cars were still suffering from the old reliability problems. Complete McLaren success and reliability were still a year away. Despite these problems, Bruce McLaren's car ran like a well-oiled clock at Mosport, and it pulled away to achieve a very popular win.

The Ford sweep at LeMans in 1966 capped a banner year for that company. Ford won the FIA Manufacturers' Prototype Championship and all of the three major endurance races (Daytona, Sebring, and LeMans) that year. The Ford Mark II, driven by Bruce McLaren and Chris Amon, won LeMans before a record crowd, as seen in this photograph.

Lothar Motschenbacher, driving a McLaren M1A (96; left front row) won the USRRC race at Mid-Ohio in August 1966. Also in the strong field are Ludwig Heimrath's McLaren M1A (39), John Cannon's McLaren M1A (62), Mark Donohue's Lola T70 (6), Chuck Parsons' McLaren M1A (10), Charlie Hayes' McLaren M1A (98), Jerry Hansen's Wolverine (88), Richard Brown's McLaren M1A (38), Ralph Salyer's McKee (25), Mak Kroon's McKee (77), Earl Jones' Genie (52), and Skip Hudson's Lola T70 (9).

Chuck Parsons won the USRRC championship in 1966. He drove a Genie during the first part of the season, before switching to a McLaren M1A (seen here) in midseason.

John Cannon's plea for mercy.

Denise McCluggage was not only a highly competent motor racing journalist during the 1960s, but an outstanding competitor as well. At the September Road America 500, Denise and Bob Grossman drove a Ferrari GTB to seventh overall.

The newly created Canadian-American Challenge Cup series made its spectacular debut at St. Jovite, Canada, on September 11, 1966. John Surtees' Lola T70 (3; left), Bruce McLaren's McLaren M1B (4; center), and Chris Amon's McLaren M1B (5) were in the front row for the start of that first race, and those three also finished in the top three spots.

John Surtees' Lola T70 (3) and Bruce McLaren's McLaren M1B (4) were never further than a few feet apart during their race for the lead at the St. Jovite race. Surtees won the race, with McLaren finishing second and Amon third.

John Surtees relaxes during practice for the Bridgehampton Can-Am race in 1966.

The radical Chaparral 2E made its first appearance at the Bridgehampton Can-Am. Two of these cars were entered for Jim Hall and Phil Hill, but only Hill started the race. (Hall was forced out with wing problems.) Hill challenged Dan Gurney for the lead, but wing problems forced him to slow down, and he finished fourth overall.

In 1966 Dan Gurney became the first American driver to win a Can-Am race at Bridgehampton. He was closely challenged by Chris Amon's McLaren M1B and won the race by barely a car length.

When the Can-Am series moved to Mosport in 1966, Mark Donohue, driving a Lola T70 (6), defeated the field to win the first Can-Am race for Penske Racing. Donohue is closely pursued by Jim Hall in a Chaparral 2E (66); Hall later dropped out of the race due to a blown engine.

Jackie Stewart (left) and Phil Hill (right) enjoy a chat during a lull in practice for the Can-Am race at Laguna Seca in October.

As competitive and innovative as they were, the Chaparrals were only a winner once in the nine-year history of the Can-Am series. That win took place at Laguna Seca in October 1966, and it resulted in a one-two sweep of the first two places on the podium. The Chaparral 2Es of Jim Hall (66) and Phil Hill (65) led a strung-out field up the hill toward Turn 1, as Bruce McLaren's McLaren M1B (4), John Surtees' Lola T70 (7), Masten Gregory's McLaren M1A (88), Mark Donohue's Lola T70 (61), Denis Hulme's Lola T70 (8), Bill Eve's Genie (52), Earl Jones' McLaren M1A (99), and Pedro Rodriguez's Ferrari Dino (21) pursue the leaders. Hill won the race, with Hall finishing second.

Dan Gurney, in a Lola T70 (30), and Chris Amon, in a McLaren M1B (5), race for fourth position early in the October 1966 race at Laguna Seca. Neither driver finished.

Chuck Parsons' McLaren M1A (1) chases three other competitors toward Turn 7 on the beautiful old Laguna Seca circuit.

Graham Hill started only one Can-Am race, driving a Team Surtees Lola T70 in the 1966 Times Grand Prix. He finished third.

Opposite: John Surtees, driving a Lola T70 (7) and Jim Hall in a Chaparral 2E (66) waged a lead-changing battle for many laps before a boiling fuel situation forced Hall to drop back and finish in second spot.

Below: Bruce McLaren (4), his McLaren M1B now using a 5.9-liter Chevrolet engine, qualified for the pole and led the first 10 laps of the Times race before his engine went off song. Jim Hall's Chaparral 2E (66) and John Surtees (7), running respectively in second and third, would engage in a classic race of their own.

The final Can-Am race of the 1966 season was held at the Stardust International Raceway in Las Vegas, Nevada. John Surtees, with his Lola T70 (7), led the field to Turn 1 on the dusty, desert circuit. Pursuing Surtees were Jim Hall's Chaparral 2E (66), Parnelli Jones' Lola T70 (98), Phil Hill's Chaparral 2E (65), Jackie Stewart's Lola T70 (43), George Follmer's Lola T70 (16), Bruce McLaren's McLaren M1B (4), Chris Amon's McLaren M1B (5), Mark Donohue's Lola T70 (6), and Masten Gregory's McLaren M1B (88). John Surtees won the race and became the first overall Can-Am champion.

Sometimes bad things happen in motor racing. Such was the case of Rodrigo Borjes, whose Ferrari 365P2 overturned and burst into flames at Nassau. Borjes was badly burned in the accident.

The legendary Nassau Speed Weeks ran for the last time in December 1966. The start of the final Nassau Trophy Race finds Skip Scott's McLaren M1B (92), Bob Grossman's Cobra 427 (6), John (Buck) Fulp's Lola T70 (26), Kenneth Duclos' Cicada Special-Chevrolet (34), and Mark Donohue's Lola T70 (7) racing toward Turn 1 after the green flag fell on the LeMans start.

A. J. Foyt, jockeying a Lola T70 (83), and Buck Fulp race for position during the Nassau Trophy Race. Foyt's Lola was powered by a 427-cid Ford engine and, in spite of severe overheating, it managed to finish 13th overall, while Fulp finished 6th overall.

Mark Donohue won the Nassau Trophy Race. Chief Mechanic Karl Kainhofer is on the far right, while Roger Penske stands behind Donohue.

Ferrari, Chaparral, and Ford were all very busy during the off-season, and as a result, several new and exciting cars were at the 24 Hours of Daytona in February 1967. Probably the most innovative and exciting entry at Daytona was the Chaparral 2F. Powered by an aluminum 427-cid Chevrolet engine, this car totally dominated the first four hours of the race before succumbing to chassis and suspension damage caused by an accident when Phil Hill hit the wall on the 88th lap.

Ferrari entered two of its beautiful new 330P4s at Daytona, supported by two private 412Ps. The 412P, with its P4 body, Campagnolo wheels, and four-liter engine, was basically an updated P3 used during the previous season. Chris Amon and Lorenzo Bandini drove this P4 to an unexpected win at Daytona.

Ford entered its updated version of the very successful Mark II that had swept all before it during the previous season. There was a serious problem, however, with the heat treating of the transmission output shafts, and that defect caused all of the factory Ford transmissions to fail. The Mark II (1) driven by Bruce McLaren and Lucien Bianchi was the only Ford to finish; it came in seventh overall.

With a sweeping victory assured, Ferrari decided to duplicate Ford's 1966 blanket finish at LeMans. This time there would be no controversy over who the winner was, since the Amon/Bandini Ferrari 330P4 (23) was three laps ahead of its nearest competitor at the finish. Mike Parkes and Ludovico Scarfiotti (24) finished second in their P4, and Pedro Rodriguez and Jean Guichet (26) finished third in their 412P.

Knowing that the Mark II was no longer competitive after the transmission failure disaster at Daytona, Ford put its full effort into completing the new Mark IV. The lighter, more powerful Mark IV made its racing debut at Sebring and was a smashing success, with Mario Andretti and Bruce McLaren driving to victory.

The USRRC was still drawing large and competitive fields in 1967, since many of the American teams were using this series to test new cars and ideas for the upcoming Can-Am season. Mark Donohue (6) dominated the eight-race series by winning six events in his Sunoco Lola T70, and he won the championship going away. Donohue leads Pierre Phillips in a Lola T70 (3) at the Laguna Seca race in May. Donohue finished 3rd and Phillips 10th.

George Follmer (16) probably had the fastest Lola T70 on the USRRC circuit, but a lack of funds and bad luck prevented him from finishing races, and he withdrew from the series after several races. At Laguna Seca, Follmer finished 17th while Mark Donohue (6) finished 3rd.

Lothar Motschenbacher (11) drove a Lola T70 in the 1967 Can-Am. He leads Ludwig Heimrath in a McLaren M1B (39) and Skip Barber in a McLaren M1B (14) during the first race of the season, at Road America in September. Barber finished 7th, Motschenbacher 9th, and Heimrath 21st.

Left: The five-year domination of the McLaren team began with Denis Hulme's win at Road America. When the six race series moved to Bridgehampton in mid-September, Hulme, driving his McLaren M6A (5), led a powerful and noisy field off of the line as Bruce McLaren's McLaren M6A (4), Mark Donohue's Lola T70 (6), Jim Hall's Chaparral 2G (66), George Follmer's Lola T70 (16), Skip Scott's M1C (91), Jerry Grant's Lola T70 (78), Dan Gurney's Lola T70 (36), John Surtees' Lola T70 (7), Chuck Parsons' M1C (26), and Peter Revson's Lola T70 (52) give chase. Hulme won his second race in a row at Bridgehampton.

Opposite: Dan Gurney and A. J. Foyt (1), the all-American team, drove their Ford Mark IV to victory at LeMans over a very strong challenge from Ferrari, Chaparral, and Porsche. Gurney leads the Ford Mark IIB of Ronnie Bucknum (57) and the Gulf Mirage-Ford of David Piper (14) during the early hours of the race. Sadly, the FIA changed the rules regarding engine displacement for the 1968 season, and this forced the withdrawal of Ford, Chaparral, and Ferrari from further endurance competition after the completion of the 1967 season.

A great illustration of the type of legendary competition that appeared during the early years of the Can-Am series. The Lola T70 of Dan Gurney (36), the McLaren M1B of Mike Spence (22), the Lola T70s of Peter Revson (52), John Surtees (8), George Follmer (16), Lothar Motschenbacher (11), and Roger McCluskey (12), and the McLaren M1B of Ludwig Heimrath (39) rush through Moss Corner during the early laps of the Mosport Can-Am.

Two of the series' top stars, Bruce McLaren in his McLaren M6A (4) and Dan Gurney in his Lola T70 (36), are in a close race for second place during the Mosport Can-Am. Gurney's Lola expired on the 69th lap, leaving McLaren to finish in second place behind teammate Denny Hulme.

Right: One of the many characters who graced the Can-Am scene. "Donald Duck Is A Speed Freak" was seen at Laguna Seca.

Opposite: Sam Posey's Caldwell D7 (1) and Ludwig Heimrath's McLaren M1B (39) charge down the Bridgehampton start-finish straight during the early part of the September Can-Am event. The Caldwell, with its driver-operated wing, was built by Ray Caldwell and financed by Sam Posey. Unfortunately, the highest placing for the Chevrolet-powered car was a 12th overall at Mosport, and the trouble-plagued venture was sidelined at the end of the season.

For many of us, Laguna Seca was one of the world's most photogenic racing circuits, and this spot between Turns 2 and 3 illustrates why. Bud Morley's Lola T70 (14), Jonathan Williams' Ferrari 300P4 (27), Bill Amick's McLaren M1C (19), John Cannon's M1B (33), and others snake their way toward Turn 3 early in the race.

Below: Bruce McLaren raises his hand in victory as he crosses the Laguna Seca finish line in October.

The McLaren team won five out of six Can-Am races in 1967 with its M6A cars. Bruce McLaren (4) won two races and became the series champion, while his teammate Denis Hulme (5) won three races and finished second in the final points standing.

Bruce McLaren claims the fruits of victory at the October 1967 Times Grand Prix. He had competed at the Riverside event since 1961, and this was his first win.

Mark Donohue led the Stardust race until he ran out of gas on the final lap. Donohue finished in a sputtering second place.

Denny Hulme (The Bear) had a strong Can-Am season. His hard-charging driving technique captured the hearts of racing fans everywhere.

Opposite: Mike Spence's McLaren M1B (22), John Surtees' Lola T70 (7), and Denis Hulme's McLaren M6A (5) battle for the lead at the Stardust International Raceway Can-Am. John Surtees won this final Can-Am race of 1967 in his year-old Lola T70. This was the only Lola victory in the series.

Porsche won its first 24-hour race at Daytona in February 1968, and the team decided to duplicate Ferrari's blanket finish from the previous year. Although it looks like the Siffert/Mitter (52) Porsche 907 is the winner, it was actually the second-place finisher, 14 laps behind the winning Elford/Neerpasch (54) Porsche 907. The Buzzetta/Schlesser (51) Porsche 907 was the third-place finisher.

Taken from the Goodyear blimp, this photograph gives a great overview of what the Le Mans start at Sebring was all about. The De Udy/Dibley Lola T70 (11) leads the front runners off of the line. Following behind are Mitter/Stommelen's Porsche 907 (48), Thompson/Lowther/Heppenstall's Howmet TX Turbine (76), Patrick/Jordan's Lola T70 (9), Hobbs/Hawkins' Ford GT40 (29), Ickx/Redman's Ford GT40 (28), Scarfiotti/Neerpasch's Porsche 907 (50), Moffat/Kwech's Shelby Mustang (32), and Foitek/Lins' Porsche 910 (56). The Hans Herrmann/Jo Siffert Porsche 907 was the overall winner.

When the final USRRC season began in Mexico City at the Autodrome on April 1, 1968, Mexican driver Moises Solana (pictured here) won the first race of the nine-race season. Skip Scott was second and Peter Revson was third.

After the final race of the 1967 Can-Am season, Roger Penske purchased Bruce McLaren's Team McLaren M6A for Mark Donohue to drive in the 1968 USRRC series. Donohue overwhelmed the competition to win the series championship for the second year in a row.

By 1968, the USRRC had pretty much become a testing series for the Can-Am, and many of the road racing professionals were losing interest in what had been a very popular series. Why did this come to pass? Perhaps it was because many of the top-notch American drivers were competing in the many other lucrative series that were available to them at that time. No one seemed interested in running the full series any more; they just wanted to appear at a particular race to test a new car or a new idea. Jim Hall appeared at two USRRC races in 1968 to test a new fuel injection system in his Chaparral 2G (66). This was his first appearance in the USRRC since the final race of the 1965 season. Hall is shown leading Lothar Motschenbacher's McLaren M6A (11) at Laguna Seca. Mark Donohue won this race.

The six-race Can-Am season started at Road America in September. Bruce McLaren's McLaren M8A (4) leads Lothar Motschenbacher's McLaren M6B (11) in an early-race battle for second place. Denny Hulme won, with McLaren finishing second and Motschenbacher sixth.

When the 1968 Can-Am series moved to Bridgehampton, Mark Donohue, with a McLaren M6B (6), upset the field to win the second Can-Am event of his career. Here, Jim Hall, driving a Chaparral 2G (66), chases Donohue to finish in second place.

Donohue and the Penske crew celebrate the Bridgehampton win. Roger Penske stands behind Donohue.

Sam Posey's Lola T160 (1) leads a group of drivers that includes Roger McCraig's McLaren M6B (55) and Jo Bonnier's McLaren M6B (9) at the Edmonton Can-Am. The Lola that Posey drove was not a competitive car, but he managed several top-10 finishes and wound up the 1968 season as the top finishing Lola driver in the final standings.

Lady Godiva made a ride through the rain-swept paddock of Laguna Seca. Unfortunately for the spectators, she wore a body suit.

Bruce McLaren has shed his goggles in an attempt to see the Laguna Seca track during the worst downpour ever experienced there on a race weekend. McLaren finished fifth and Mark Donohue, driving a McLaren M6B (6), finished eighth.

John Cannon (62) was able to get a set of Firestone rain tires for his three-year-old McLaren M1B. Those tires, and some outstanding driving, gave Cannon one of the most popular upset victories in the history of the Can-Am series. Brian O'Neil's Lola T160 (15) trails Cannon.

Charlie Hayes' McKee Mark 7 (25) leads Lothar Motschenbacher's McLaren M6B (11) and Dan Gurney's Lola T160 (48) onto the mile-long back straight during the Times Grand Prix at Riverside. Motschenbacher finished fourth, while Hayes and Gurney failed to finish.

Bruce McLaren became the first man to win the Times Grand Prix two years in a row.

Leading the starting field into Turn 1 at Stardust International Raceway in November 1968 are the McLaren M8As of Denis Hulme (5) and Bruce McLaren (4), the Chaparral 2G of Jim Hall (66), the McLaren M6B of Peter Revson (52), and the Lola T160s of Sam Posey (1) and Dan Gurney (48). This was the final Can-Am race of the year, and Denis Hulme won it along with the series championship.

When the 11-race Can-Am series began at Mosport in June 1969, the McLaren team debuted the McLaren M8B. This car became the most dominant car in the history of the series by winning all 11 of the races.

Opposite, top: One of the biggest upset wins in the history of endurance racing took place at Daytona in February 1969, when the Penske Racing Lola T70 Mark 3B, driven by Mark Donohue and Chuck Parsons, beat a strong starting field to the finish line. This particular race was a true test of a team's endurance, since every top competitor suffered some type of serious problem, and only the most ingenious and tenacious teams survived.

Opposite, bottom: At Sebring, the Gulf Ford GT40 (22) of Jackie Oliver and Jacky Ickx won a race-long battle with the new factory Ferarri 312P. The Ford was victorious by only one lap.

The Redman/Siffert Porsche 908 (1) leads the Servoz-Gavin/Rodriguez Matra 650 (9), Bonnier/Meuller Lola T70 Mark 3B (11), Dean/Elford Porsche 908 (4), Lins/Buzzetta Porsche 908 (2), Kellerneer/Jost Ford GT40 (7), Guichet/Widdows Matra 650 (10), Ickx/Oliver Gulf Mirage M3 (5), DeLorenzo/Lang Corvette (14), and the Thompson/Morrison Corvette (15) off the starting line at the Watkins Glen 6-Hour race. The Porsche team swept the first three places, with Brian Redman and Jo Siffert taking the overall victory.

Opposite: In spite of qualifying in fourth position, John Surtees, driving a McLaren M12 (7), got a great start at St. Jovite and beat Lothar Motschenbacher's McLaren M12 (11), Bruce McLaren's McLaren M8B (4), Chuck Parsons' Lola T163 (10), and Denis Hulme's McLaren M8B (5) into the first turn. Surtees, McLaren, and Hulme swapped the top three positions for many laps until Surtees and McLaren tangled with each other as they lapped a back marker who wasn't watching his mirrors. Hulme won the race, while McLaren finished second and Surtees did not finish.

Right: A sign of times past. Members of the Chaparral and McLaren teams help replace the engine in one of their competitor's cars. Chuck Parsons' Lola T163 was the recipient of his rivals' generosity, but a water leak put him out of contention early in the race.

You can almost hear the roar of several thousand horsepower as you look at this starting lineup of Can-Am cars at Mid-Ohio. Bruce McLaren (4) and Denis Hulme (5) both in McLaren M8Bs, Mark Donohue's Lola T163 (6), Chuck Parsons' Lola T163 (10), John Surtees' Chaparral 2H (7), George Eaton's McLaren M12 (98), Jo Siffert's Porsche 917PA (0), Peter Revson's Lola T163 (31), and Lothar Motschenbacher's McLaren M12 (11) await the fall of the green flag. Hulme won the race.

These two cars (McLaren M8Bs) were so good that it was a foregone conclusion that one of them would win the race. It was just a matter of which one it would be, Hulme (5) or McLaren (4), or on occasion Gurney or Amon.

Chuck Parsons' Lola T163 (10) leads Tony Dean's Porsche 908 (8) and Mario Andretti's McLaren M6B (1) into Turn 9 at Laguna Seca. Parsons finished third, Andretti fourth, and Dean seventh.

Bruce McLaren takes the checkered flag at Laguna Seca, as teammate Denis Hulme follows close behind. McLaren also won the 1969 series championship.

As Mario Andretti heads into Turn 9 at Laguna Seca, one can see the huge crowds that were attracted to the Can-Am races in the early years of the series.

Jackie Oliver was one of the few drivers who had the right equipment to challenge the McLarens. Unfortunately, Peter Bryant's Ti22 did not have the sponsorship, or the budget, to really push the car to its maximum capacity.

The End of an Era

The 1970 professional sports car racing season is memorable for two events, one triumphant and the other tragic. First were the incredible endurance battles waged between the Porsche 917 and the Ferrari 512, giving endurance racing fans something special to whet their appetites for the first time in years. Porsche had done its homework since the 917's debut in mid-1969. The car's aerodynamic problems had, for the most part, been cured, and the engine had undergone extensive testing during the 1969 Can-Am season. When the revised 917 made its debut at Daytona in February 1970, the car's performance did not disappoint the many Porsche fans who turned out to see it run. At the end of the 24-hour race, the Porsches finished in the first two spots. The new Ferrari 512 finished in third spot at Daytona but would soon gain its redemption at Sebring. The finish of the 1970 Sebring race was the closest in the history of that event, with the Mario Andretti/Ignazio Giunti/Nino Vaccarella Ferrari 512 coming from

Two of endurance racing's most legendary cars—the Ferrari 512S and the Porsche 917—made their American debut at Daytona in February 1970, and this was the result. The Andretti/Merzario/Ickx Ferrari 512S (28) and the Siffert/Redman Porsche 917 (1) race around the fourth turn banking, wheel-to-wheel, at 220 miles per hour. Meanwhile, the Porsche 917s of Rodriguez/Kinnunen (2) and Elford/Ahrens (3) follow in close pursuit. Pedro Rodriguez and Leo Kinnunen won the race, while Brian Redman and Jo Siffert came in second. The Ferrari of Mario Andretti, Jacky Ickx, and Arturo Merzario finished third, and Vic Elford/Kurt Ahrens did not finish.

behind to defeat the Steve McQueen/Peter Revson Porsche 908 by 22.1 seconds. Porsche finally secured its first LeMans victory after several heartbreaking misses and also won the Watkins Glen 6-Hour race, the third FIA Manufacturers' Championship race, and the World Manufacturers' Championship.

When the Can-Am season opened at Mosport in June 1970, one of the most radical of all Can-Am cars was seen for the first time. The AVS Shadow Mark 1 (16) driven by George Follmer looked more like a go-cart than a big-bore racing car. With its specially made 10-inch front and 12-inch rear Firestone tires and its low-slung body, theoretically the car should have worked. In practice, however, the car was a failure, and Follmer, followed by Vic Elford, walked away from the project. After competing in 4 of the 10 races in the series, the Shadow was parked for the remainder of the season. Here, George Follmer leads Gordon Dewar's McLaren M6A (47), Oscar Koveleski's McLaren M8B (54), Bob Dini's Lola T163 (75), and Ron Goldleaf's McLaren M6B (17) before overheating forced Follmer to retire early in the race.

The second significant event in 1970 was a tragic one. On June 2, 1970, just 12 days before the start of the Can-Am season, defending champion Bruce McLaren was killed at Goodwood during the final testing of his company's all-new M8D Group 7 car. This tragedy did not cripple the McLaren Can-Am effort, however, and drivers Dan Gurney, Denis Hulme, and Peter Gethin managed to win 9 of the 10 races on the schedule. Hulme won the championship.

The 1971 season was an almost a complete rerun of the previous one, with Porsche and Ferrari continuing their dynamic battle for the Manufacturers' Championship, which Porsche once again won. Sadly, after the finish of the 1971 endurance season, the five-liter cars were relegated to the scrap heap by FIA rules changes. It always seemed that just as things got exciting, the FIA would stupidly step in, change the rules, and everything would return to square one.

A great upset almost took place at Sebring in March 1970 when the privately entered Porsche 908 driven by Steve McQueen and Peter Revson came within seconds of beating all of the factory-backed Ferraris and Porsches. Were it not for an extremely heroic effort by Mario Andretti, driving a Ferrari 512S, McQueen and Revson would have won the race. As it was, they finished second overall and first in class.

McLaren dominated the Can-Am season by winning 8 of the 10 races. For the first time in the history of the series, an American, Peter Revson, won the championship. The Lola team, with Jackie Stewart driving the T260, seemed poised to challenge McLaren's domination of the Can-Am series, but that effort fizzled after two early season victories, due to various handling problems.

By 1972, three-liter cars were competing for the World Manufacturers' Championship, which went to the incredible Ferrari 312PB for winning all 12 of the races that it entered that year. The only race that escaped the Ferrari onslaught was LeMans, and that was because the factory posted no entries due to political problems. Matra won that race.

When the FIA changed the Manufacturers' Championship rules, Porsche changed direction and put its full racing effort into the lucrative Can-Am series. At the 1972 series premier at Mosport on June 11, Mark Donohue, and Penske Racing, were there in a new Porsche 917/10K. This car was powered by a turbocharged 917 engine, and with it, Donohue and George Follmer won six of the nine races slated that year. Follmer became the second American to win the Can-Am championship. The McLaren team withdrew from the Can-Am series at the end of the season, even though the marque had won three of the nine races. It was a case of the reasonably small McLaren operation not being able to match Porsche's overwhelming factory superiority. After the competition of the 1972 professional sports car season, the Can-Am series went into a downhill spin and never fully recovered.

The 1973 Daytona 24-Hour race was to be the last one run as a world championship competition. Peter Gregg and Hurley Haywood, driving a Porsche RS, won that race. Sebring had been dropped from the international racing calendar because the track management had not been able to upgrade the facility to FIA specifications. The Watkins Glen 6-Hour race remained on the FIA calendar in 1973 and 1974, and Matra won both of those events.

An upstart organization, IMSA (International Motor Sports Association), had been formed by John Bishop in 1969. IMSA, with its sponsorship from Camel, was to become an extremely popular and very competitive racing series from 1973 until the early 1990s when politics and unpopular rules changes chased the factory participation away and destroyed the organization. In 1973, Sebring ran their 12-hour race as an IMSA event and in 1974, the Daytona 24-Hour race also became an IMSA event. These two races became the cornerstone of what was to become a terrific racing series.

Porsche came into the 1973 Can-Am series with a brand-new car, the super powerful 917/30, and that car swept to victory in six of the eight races, with Mark Donohue at the wheel. By the end of that Can-Am season, Porsche had achieved its goal of winning the series two years in a row and officially withdrew from the series. By 1973, the Can-Am series was dying a fast death, because of the high cost of staying competitive and the lack of interest of track organizers; and after only five of eight races in 1974, the patient died. The only major team to compete in 1974 was the UOP Shadow team, which won four of the five races in that abbreviated season, with Jackie Oliver becoming the final Can-Am champion.

With the death of the Can-Am series, the final straw was broken in what many people consider to be the greatest period of American professional sports car racing. Why was this such a great era? I thinks the answer lies in the fact that so many great cars, drivers, and circuits were involved in professional sports car racing at the same time. It was also a time in which racing wasn't completely overrun by uncaring corporate sponsors and dictatorial television networks. It was also a time in which camaraderie and friendship mattered above all else and it was a time when the public could interact with the drivers. That is what made this the golden age of sports car racing.

In July 1970, well-orchestrated pit stops such as this helped Pedro Rodriguez (bottom right) and Leo Kinnunen (bottom left) achieve victory in their Gulf Porsche 917 at the Watkins Glen 6-Hour race.

After Bruce McLaren was tragically killed in a testing accident just weeks prior to the start of the 1970 Can-Am season, Dan Gurney, a longtime friend, stepped forward to join Denis Hulme on the McLaren team. Gurney won the first two races of the year at Mosport and St. Jovite, but he ran out of luck when his engine overheated at Watkins Glen, where he finished ninth. Unfortunately, Gurney left the McLaren team after Watkins Glen because of a conflict in oil company sponsorships.

Opposite, top: British F5000 Champion Peter Gethin took Gurney's spot on the McLaren team for the rest of the 1970 season. The pint-sized Gethin looked lost in the cockpit of the M8D that was set up for a much taller man, but he soon acclimated himself enough to win at Road America and finish third overall in the final standings.

Opposite, bottom: The Lola T220, driven by Peter Revson, was heralded as a serious challenger to the dynasty that the McLaren team had established in the Can-Am. However, its numerous untested shortcomings soon became apparent, and the best finish that was achieved by the Lola was a second at Road America.

Chris Amon, driving a March 707 (77), and Jackie Oliver, in a Bryant Ti22 Mark 2 (22), challenge Denis Hulme's McLaren M8D down the famous corkscrew at Laguna Seca. Oliver and Hulme staged the closest nose-to-tail battle of the entire season until late in the race, when minor engine problems caused a slight loss of power in Oliver's car. He finished a very close second.

Denis Hulme receives congratulations from Peter Bryant (far left) and Jackie Oliver (second from left) after his exciting win at Laguna Seca. Stirling Moss is standing behind Hulme, who won 6 out of the 10 Can-Am races in 1970 and was the runaway winner of the series championship.

Vic Elford receives last-minute instructions from Jim Hall before taking the most controversial car ever seen in the Can-Am out for practice. The Chaparral 2J pushed all of the boundaries of automotive engineering and design to the absolute limit at that time. Hall's reward for his progressive thinking was to have the car banned from further competition by the FIA at the end of the 1970 season.

Mark Donohue and David Hobbs gave the Porsche 917s all of the competition that they never wanted with their beautifully prepared and extremely fast Ferrari 512M. The Penske Racing-owned car made its debut at Daytona in February 1971 and led the first part of the race until electrical troubles and a collision with a back marker forced it into long pit stops for repairs. In spite of these problems, the Ferrari finished third overall. Here, the Donohue/Hobbs Ferrari 512M (6) leads the winning Porsche 917K (2) of Jackie Oliver and Pedro Rodriguez into the final turn before climbing up onto the Daytona banking.

Below: The Elford/Van Lennep Porsche 197K (3) and the Rodriguez/Oliver Porsche 917K are neck-and-neck at 220-plus miles per hour around the fourth turn of the Daytona banking. After running near the front for much of the race, the Martini–Rossi–sponsored car was involved in a collision that put it out of the race. Elford's luck would be better at Sebring, where he and Gerald Larrousse gave the Martini team a well-deserved win.

Denis Hulme won three races, at Mosport, Edmonton, and Riverside, in his McLaren M8F. Hulme's numerous other podium finishes during the 10-race series helped him finish second in the final Can-Am Standings.

In 1971, Lola seemed poised to challenge the dominant McLarens for the Can-Am title. The Lola T260 driven by Jackie Stewart won the second and fifth races of the season at St. Jovite and Mid-Ohio, but serious handling problems prevented the car from taking any more wins. Two second places at Edmonton and Laguna Seca helped Stewart finish third overall in the final championship standings.

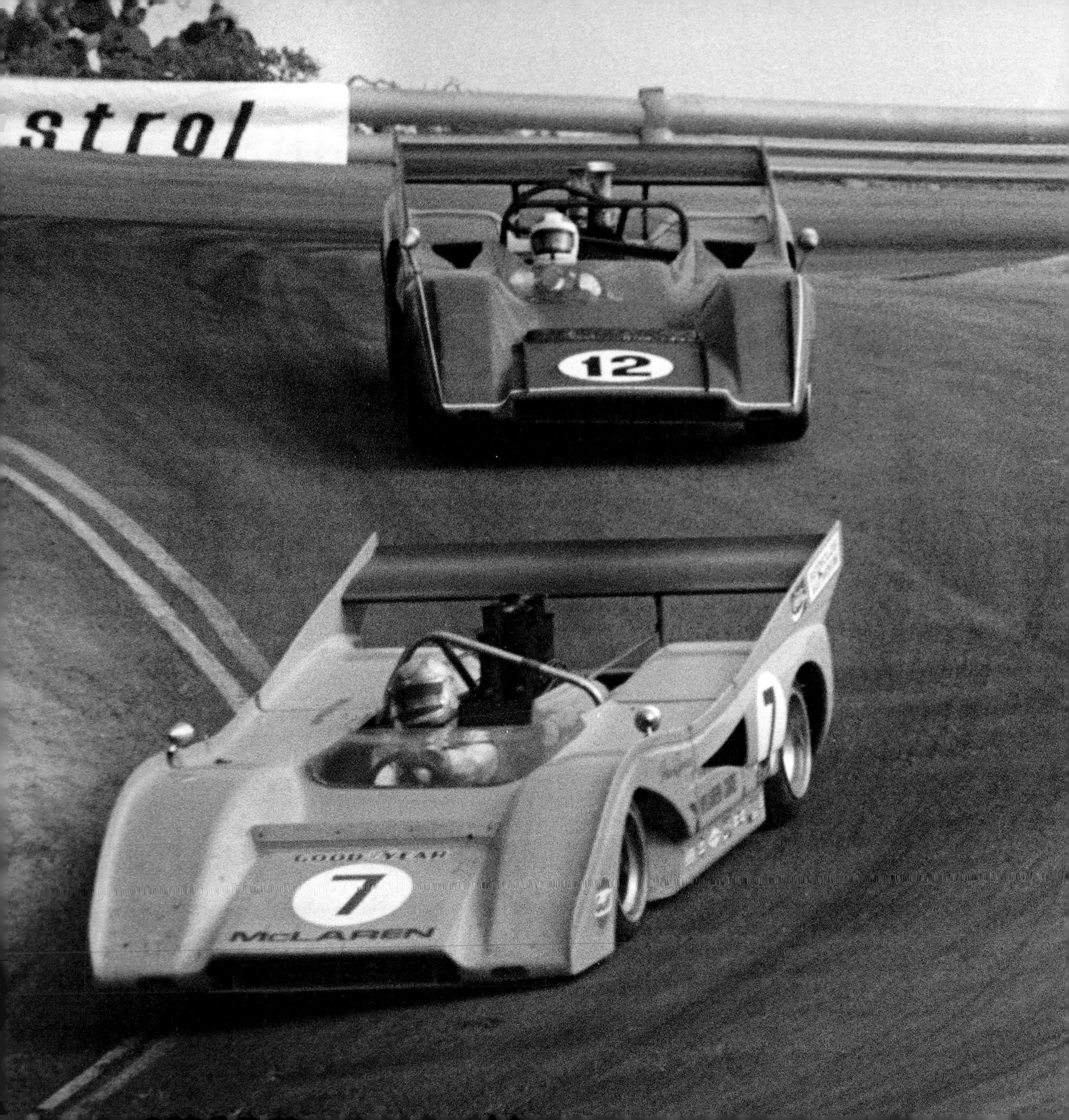
strol
12
GOOD YEAR
7
McLAREN

Peter Revson, now driving for the McLaren team, finally realized the success that he so well deserved in the Can-Am series. In 1971, Revson won 5 of the 10 races, including this one at Laguna Seca, where he led Chuck Parsons' McLaren M8E (12) down the corkscrew. Revson also became the first American to win the Can-Am championship.

Three other contenders during the 1971 Can-Am season were Jackie Oliver, driving a Shadow Mark 2 (101), Brian Redman in a BRM P167 (38), and Jo Siffert in a Porsche 917/10 (20). At Laguna Seca, Redman finished fourth and Siffert fifth, while Oliver failed to finish due to throttle linkage problems.

Peter Revson, 1971 Can-Am champion. He was winner at Road Atlanta, Watkins Glen, Road America, Donnybrooke, and Laguna Seca.

In 1972, Jacky Ickx and Mario Andretti, driving their Ferrari 312PB (85), won all three of the FIA endurance races run on American soil—Daytona, Sebring, and Watkins Glen. That car was so successful in 1972 that it won all 12 of the endurance races in which it was entered, plus the FIA World Manufacturers' Championship. At Watkins Glen, Andretti leads Brian Redman's Ferrari 312PB (87), Gijs Van Lennep's Gulf Mirage (20), and Gerald Larrousse's Lola T280 (90) early in the race.

The 1972 Can-Am season will always be remembered for the dominating performances of the Penske Racing Porsche 917/10Ks, but it didn't start out that way. At Mosport in June and again at Watkins Glen In July, Denis Hulme upset the apple cart with his McLaren M20. But in spite of everything that Hulme and teammate Peter Revson tried to do, the McLarens were finally overmatched by the turbocharged Porsches. Regrettably, the McLaren team withdrew from the series at the end of the season.

Popular French driver François Cevert, driving a McLaren M8F (22), was the only other McLaren driver to win a Can-Am race in 1972. He won in September at Donnybrooke, in Brainerd, Minnesota.

Mark Donohue (6) and George Follmer (7) won six of the nine Can-Am races during the 1972 season in their Porsche 917/10Ks. Donohue crashed, breaking his leg, during a testing session at Road Atlanta in early July, and Roger Penske flew George Follmer in at the last minute to take Donohue's place during his recovery. Follmer was up to the assignment and won the Road Atlanta race in spite of having very little familiarization time in the new Porsche. By the time Donohue was ready to return to the cockpit at Donnybrooke in September, Follmer had already won three races and was leading in championship points. Penske decided to run two cars and retain both drivers for the rest of the year.

George Follmer became the second American to win the Can-Am Championship. He did it by winning five of the nine series races in 1972: 1, Road Atlanta; 2, Mid-Ohio; 3, Road America; 4, Laguna Seca; 5, Riverside.

Certainly one of the most interesting engine experiments to be tried during the 1972 season was the Shadow Team's twin-turbocharged Chevrolet. Rumored to put out nearly 1,200 horsepower, the engine could not be made race-ready and was only practiced at Riverside by NASCAR star Bobby Allison.

In 1973, Porsche introduced its new 2.8-liter Carrera RS to racing at Daytona. The car was so new that it had to run in the sports car category instead of in the GT class due to the lack of the required numbers for homologation. Mark Donohue and George Follmer drove this Sunoco-Penske-entered Carrera into the lead, but the car collapsed a piston after 14 hours and was retired from the race.

The Porsche 917/30 was probably the finest overall Can-Am car ever built. What a pity that the car didn't have any real competition in 1973, so that it could show what it could do when pushed to the limit. Of the eight Can-Am races run in 1973, Mark Donohue won six straight after having difficulties in the first two races at Mosport and Road Atlanta.

Index